CULTURE
AND
AFRICAN
AMERICAN POLITICS

BLACKS IN THE DIASPORA

DARLENE CLARK HINE, JOHN MCCLUSKEY, JR., AND
DAVID BARRY GASPAR

GENERAL EDITORS

CULTURE
AND
AFRICAN
AMERICAN POLITICS

CHARLES P. HENRY

INDIANA UNIVERSITY PRESS
Bloomington and Indianapolis

Manufactured in the United States of America

Library of Congress Cataloging-in-Publication Data

Henry, Charles P.
Culture and African American politics / Charles P. Henry.
p.   cm.—(Blacks in the diaspora)
Includes bibliographical references.
ISBN 0-253-32754-7
1. Afro-Americans—Politics and government. 2. Political culture—
United States—History—20th century. 3. United States—Politics
and government—1981-1989. I. Title. II. Series: Blacks in the
diaspora series.
E185.615.H365 1990
305.8'96073—dc20   88-46100

1 2 3 4 5 94 93 92 91 90   CIP

*To my mother, Ruth, and to
the memory of my father, Charles*

CONTENTS

Preface

Having begun my study of politics during the crucial years when civil rights protests were transformed into black power demands, I was naturally attracted to the issues of identity, ideology, and people power. On entering graduate school, I found no political science courses relating these phenomena to the black experience in a significant way. There were courses in black literature, black theology, and black history—I took the maximum number allowable—that demonstrated that blacks had thought about such issues. Yet such thought was seldom linked in a direct way to political philosophy or political behavior.

The works of such scholars as John Blassingame, James Cone, and Lawrence Levine have been influential in revealing a historic black community that maintained a distinctive moral and social life. Their use of such folk sources as spirituals, folktales, and sermons has been instrumental in my search for the roots of contemporary black political behavior. My own use of such sources has taken me far from my professional training. Thus, this study is written with the hope that it can become a building block for those with more relevant training and keener insight.

Many people have provided me with assistance and encouragement with this endeavor over nearly a decade. The initial stages of this work were completed with the support of Denison University and the wise counsel of William Nichols and Jack Kirby. A post-doctoral fellowship from the National Endowment for the Humanities enabled me to spend a year at Atlanta University broadening my knowledge of the humanities and music under the guidance of Richard Long. Finally, my move to the University of California at Berkeley brought me into contact with a wide range of scholars who were helpful in shaping this work. These scholars and others who read all or parts of the book include Earl Lewis, Dianne Pinderhughes, Matthew Holden, William Nelson, Frances Smith Foster, Bertram Gross, Aaron Wildavsky, and Ron Takaki. I am indebted to them for their thoughtful advice and encouragement. Of course, the views expressed in this work are solely my own.

My appreciation goes to the University of California for several summer grants and to the staff of the Afro-American Studies Department for their technical help—especially Cheryl Pittman. I owe a special thanks to general series editor Darlene Clark Hine. Finally, the life of the mind would be incomplete without the love and support of my family. My wife, Loretta, and my children, Adia, Wes, and Laura, are reflected in this book in ways that only I know, yet their contribution is nonetheless real.

CULTURE
AND
AFRICAN
AMERICAN POLITICS

CHAPTER

1

IDEOLOGY, POLITICS, AND CULTURE

> But can a people (its faith in an idealized American Creed notwithstanding) live and develop for over three hundred years simply by reacting? Are American Negroes simply the creation of white men, or have they at least helped to create themselves out of what they found around them?
>
> Men have made a way of life in caves and upon cliffs, why cannot Negroes have made a life upon the horns of white man's dilemma.
>
> —Ralph Ellison
>
> America was founded on a belief in God—and I don't care what it is . . .
>
> —Dwight D. Eisenhower

Any attempt to communicate—whether written, oral, or visual—is fraught with danger. Attempts at communication between racial groups are especially dangerous. Yet individuals and groups must communicate to survive. During the civil rights movement one often heard the question: What does the Negro want? After a decade of demonstrations, protests, and marches, the question was no longer asked. Instead one heard: The Negro has got too much! To many blacks, however, such questions and reactions were absurd. No one could speak for all blacks. Moreover, few blacks believed that they had too much of anything that really mattered.

The man who spoke for more Afro-Americans than anyone else, Martin Luther King, Jr., believed Negroes and whites had fundamentally different definitions of the term "equality":

> Negroes have proceeded from a premise that equality means what it says, and they have taken white Americans at their word when they talked of it as an objective. But most whites in America in 1967, including many persons of

1

goodwill, proceed from a premise that equality is a loose expression for improvement. White America is not even psychologically organized to close the gap—essentially it seeks only to make it less painful and less obvious but in most respects to retain it. Most abrasions between Negroes and white liberals arise from this fact. (King 1967b, 8)

In *Where Do We Go from Here?* King went on to condemn many liberals who clung to the traditional ideas of equal opportunity and equal treatment instead of promoting new concepts like affirmative action.

Obviously, King and the white liberals he spoke of were on different wave lengths. While it would be impossible to level all differences, King definitely had in mind something more than the limited equality offered—especially in a society that had done so much to make the conditions between the races unequal. Yet it should have come as no surprise to King that terms like "equality," "democracy," and "freedom" are conditional. In ancient Greece, the classic model of a political society, "freedom" meant primarily the independence of the city-state, not any high degree of personal liberty. According to classics scholar Russell Kirk:

The Athenian democracy had been rash, selfish, and merciless, devastating even neutral states; Athens' immense resources had been squandered in extravagant undertakings, and the Athenian people had elavated to leadership demagogues and self-seeking adventurers, while exiling or rejecting or misemploying those men of integrity and ability who might have saved the polis. (Kirk 1974, 71)

Given Athenian "democracy," it is small wonder that Socrates was forced to drink hemlock. Given American "democracy," it is small wonder that King was assassinated.

King and his supporters were attempting to force white Americans to live up to the "American Creed."[1] King, however, had a different conception of what that creed entailed than did most white Americans. To the extent that black and white perceptions were congruent, King was successful. But the differences in those perceptions proved fatal to both King and the civil rights movement.

We contend that the differing racial perceptions of the meaning of the basic ideals of a political system is essentially an ideological problem. If we define ideology as a system of cultural symbols, widely shared, which articulate ethical principles and justify political action,[2] then we must examine the ways in which culture mediates political meaning. We propose to do this by examining several questions: What values have traditionally been expressed in black mass culture (subculture)? Do these values form a belief system or ideology that significantly influences mass behavior? Has this behavior been reflected in and in turn been shaped by black institutions? Can traditional mass values be shaped into effective political ideology by black elites? These questions present a number of serious methodological and conceptual problems that have either been obscured or ignored in the literature. Moreover, any attempt to properly address them will pose a significant challenge to traditional scholarship.

A REVIEW OF THE LITERATURE

Any review of the existing literature on Afro-American political thought is necessarily brief. Although the volume of material concerning Afro-American political behavior is vast,[3] the authors of these works have generally concerned themselves with socialization, leadership, organizations, or public policy. These few devoting any attention to ideology have focused on differences between black beliefs—invariably at the elite level (e.g., DuBois' double consciousness)—or stressed that black political thought, like black culture, is derivative from the dominant ideology.

Among the early attempts to differentiate between black ideologies we find an emphasis on political style and a tendency to categorize black political leadership on that basis (Bunche 1935; Myrdal 1948; Johnson 1937; Gosnell 1967; Kelly Miller 1968).[4] Later works, while reflecting a new interest in structural contexts like institutional racism, have also tended to focus on leadership style (Wilson 1960; Gilliam 1975; Marable 1983). Several of the more recent examinations of black ideology develop certain themes that their authors see as characteristic of these ideologies. White racism is viewed as the unifying element of an ideology whose major characteristic is its concern with moral right and inclusion (Holden 1973; Storing 1970; Dolbeare and Dolbeare 1971; Boxill 1984).

The development of black studies as an academic field has led to the production of several introductory textbooks on "black politics." The authors of these books seldom define the term "black politics." Lucius J. Barker and Jesse J. McCorry, Jr., in *Black Americans and the Political System,* take the traditional approach of viewing black politics as the "American Dilemma" positing values against behavior. While they use the term "black nation" to describe the norms, dynamics, and interactions of various groups and institutions within the black community that constitute its political system, they limit themselves to a discussion of strategies within that community. A more radical approach is taken by Manning Marable in *Black American Politics.* Marable defines black politics as the racial politics of class struggle, and the pursuit of power in monopoly capitalist and colonial capitalist societies (1985, 2). Although Marable recognizes a separate and distinct national black culture and the centrality of racial categories over and above social class in the U.S., his perspective remains class-based. Ironically, his limited discussion of black culture tends to focus on black elites or the petty bourgeoisie.

Milton Morris's *The Politics of Black America* is perhaps the most comprehensive treatment of the subject. While Morris himself does not define "black politics," he describes several approaches to the topic as well as several definitions of race. He views black political attitudes as the product of *a distinct political subculture*. Moreover, he states that "the feelings of individuals or groups toward the political system is perhaps the most crucial attitudinal dimension" (p. 124). Despite this stated centrality and the recognition that black attitudes are not static, Morris limits his exploration to "several piecemeal studies that vary widely in quality." Thus, the feelings produced by the black subculture are confined to a few opinion surveys of the last twenty years.

A more recent contribution to the field of black politics by Hanes Walton (1985) suffers from the same limitations as Morris's work. Walton says that black political behavior is informed by unique forces that do not form the basis of all American political behavior because it is rooted in the black experience in America. While Walton condemns the bias of behaviorism in viewing mass political beliefs, he does little to reveal the "unique forces" that distinguish black political actions.

By looking only at leadership styles and the politics of inclusion or exclusion, these studies miss the depth and complexity of black political thought. They move from cause (racism) to consequence (behavior) without examining the interaction of symbols. There are two components of symbolic communication—content and form. Content analysis gives us the "what" but not the "how" of the subject under investigation. Scholars examining black political thought see content that is similar to the general beliefs expressed in the American creed. By turning, then, to an analysis of black style, they imply cultural differences in communication without really explaining the significances of those differences for ideology and behavior. "Content is inferred, form is observed," says Hugh Duncan, "[t]he 'factuality' of social relationship is its form, *not* its content" (Duncan 1968, 72). Thus Max Weber holds that status and class must be studied as a style (as well as a content) of social experience.

Cultural anthropologist Clifford Geertz states the question another way. It is not the truth that varies with social, psychological, and cultural contexts, says Geertz, "but the symbols we construct in our unequally effective attempts to grasp it."[5] Yet the emotive, metaphoric language of many ideologies is often viewed by social scientists as an attempt to evade reality rather than grasp it. As Geertz notes, many of our leading social theorists are incapable of a nonevaluative conception of ideology (Shils 1958; Parsons 1959; Feuer 1975; Sutton 1956; Mannheim 1936). This failure is the product of theoretical clumsiness rather than methodological indiscipline. If we are to use ideology as an analytic concept, we must go beyond the myths and rationalizations of ideology to recognize that they are "maps of problematic social reality and matrices for the creation of collective conscience" (Geertz 1973, 220). As such they draw as much if not more "from popular culture than from high art and formal religious ritual" (ibid., 216).

The tasks of science and ideology, although different, are not incompatible. Martin Luther King believed that social science might profitably examine the areas of Negro leadership, political action, and the psychological and ideological changes in Negroes (King in Brigham and Weisbach 1972, 332). Our task is descriptive, while that of the ideologue is prescriptive. This does not mean that we are not all ideologues, for we all operate within established patterns of cultural meaning. Yet if we can more clearly understand what these patterns are and how they work and what causes them, we might better critically evaluate the prescriptions they offer.

THE PROBLEM OF INTERPRETATION

Interpreting the meaning of Afro-American political thought in the United States presents at least two major obstacles. One obstacle is a general social science bias in looking at mass belief systems nonjudgmentally. The political views of the masses are seen as fragmentary, irrational, and derivative. Extreme proponents of this school would limit political participation to an educated elite. If we can surmount the elite bias in viewing mass ideology, we confront a particular problem in viewing black ideology. Elite blacks often reflect elements of the dominant white belief system and the black subculture. Folk thought, while more isolated from the mainstream, is often oral and fluid. Its constant creation and recreation are a real challenge to any observer.

The obfuscation of black ideology derives from both conservative and radical sources. Social scientists like Philip Converse and others who focus on opinion survey research argue that ideology is almost exclusively the product of an educated elite (10 percent of the U.S. population). As one moves away from the "talented tenth," beliefs become less abstract and more narrow in interest.[6] Therefore, elites who attempt to communicate with the "least informed" members of society will experience the widest divergency from elite ideology—mass beliefs (Converse in Apter 1964, 248–49). In crisis situations the masses are especially ripe for unpredictable behavior. It is just such situations that the creators of the "authoritarian personality" hope to avoid by discouraging mass participation in politics.

Marxism, on the other hand, has encouraged mass political participation. Marx's negative view of doctrine as "false consciousness" had to be modified by Lenin to give politics a more central place in Communist doctrine. However, mass political participation was always to be guided by an elite—the party. Marxism, then, like capitalism, tended to build ideology from the top down (Gouldner 1970).

Expanding on the work of Italian theorist Antonio Gramsci, historian George Rude provides us with a concept that links mass and elite beliefs. Contending that there is no such thing as spontaneous rebellion, Rude traces the development of popular ideology during the English, French, and American revolutions. He claims that such an ideology is really a fusion of two elements.

> Of these, the first is what I call the "inherent," traditional element—a sort of "mother's milk" ideology, based on direct experience, oral tradition or folk memory and not learned by listening to sermons or speeches or reading books. In this fusion the second element is the stock of ideas and beliefs that are "derived" or borrowed from others, often taking the form of a more structured system of ideas, political or religious, such as the Rights of Man, Popular Sovereignty, *Laissez-faire* and the Sacred Right of Property, Nationalism, Socialism, or the various versions of justification by Faith. (Rude 1980, 28)

Thus Rude believes that the masses are not *tabulae rasae* waiting to be written on, nor are derived ideologies necessarily superior to inherent ideologies. They often overlap, with the derived ideologies of one generation becoming a part of the inherent ideologies of the next generation. Inherent ideologies are more intuitive and immediate. Family and peer groups play a vital role in their transmission. Derived ideologies are more formal and distant. They rely on institutions like schools and churches for their transmission. While inherent ideologies are more original, Gramsci and Rude believe that mass beliefs must be combined with external ideologies of certain sympathetic elites (intellectuals) to be truly progressive or revolutionary.

If intellectuals are to work productively with the masses, the language used must have meaning for both. Political theorist Sheldon Wolin states that all political theory is linked to experience, because even the most specialized vocabularies rely on everyday language to express their meanings in the early stages of development (Wolin 1960, 15). Sociologist Alvin Gouldner details this process of development as applied to ideology:

> Ideology is grounded in the utilization of an ordinary language, but it is the restructuring of an ordinary language in special ways: partly by selectively focusing the ordinary language on certain public projects; partly by changing certain of the meanings of ordinary language, giving it a somewhat new or extraordinary meaning, extended redefinition, or focusing; partly by taking certain parts of ordinary language and making them newly problematical, thus assigning a new significance to them; partly by the invention of new signs. (Gouldner, 1976, 81)

Gouldner, then, along with Rude, Gramsci, Wolin, and Geertz, has a more positive view of ideology than those social theorists who base their views on voting studies and opinion research.

These theorists with more positive views of ideology recognize that a truly public social science cannot be value-free. In fact, it bears a strong resemblance to the predecessor of today's social sciences—moral philosophy. Yet while many early students of ideology focused on its theoretical or doctrinal logicality and truth, its pure form as set on paper was seldom manifested in the "real" world. Cultural anthropologists have been more intent on linking a system of beliefs to specific behavioral organizations. However, their studies have often been limited to a few individuals or to "primitive," isolated groups. More recently political psychology and sociology have assumed the task of establishing empirical referents for ideology in complex societies (Szalay et al. 1972 and 1983). Still, their methods of measuring "psychocultural" distance and psychological meanings are limited to a set number of test subjects in a controlled environment. For our task we must turn to those meanings that have survived over several generations and are revealed in traditional folk sources.

The eighteenth-century German philosopher, historian, and folklorist Johann Gottfried von Herder provided insight into the link between ideology, mass participation, and culture. Herder's work was prompted by the lack of a distinctly German literary tradition. This lack, Herder determined, was due to the domination of Latin over the German language, the impact of the Renaissance and the Enlightenment, and the subservience of German writers to the French literary tradition.[7] In short, the influence of derived ideologies and traditions had prevented Germany from utilizing its own culture.

Herder claimed that the deepest insight into any culture, whether ancient or modern, could be gained by examining the culture's folk tradition—even if that tradition was only secondary to the dominant one. His approach suggested the radical notion that every culture is unique and that there can be no real possibility of normative evaluation or ranking of societies. As radical as Herder's conception was, it had more of an empirical base in reality than the arguments of philosophers like Newton and Locke who, at crucial points, had to rely on affirmations of faith. The idea of natural rights had no basis in history, but every culture produced a folk ideology. For Herder, folk tradition was the agent for accomplishing linguistic change, and even more, for revolutionizing the cultural values of the society (Bluestein 1972, 6–12).

BLACK IDEOLOGY AND THE ORAL TRADITION

The search for a black ideology must begin with the oral tradition and must encompass all types of black beliefs. Like their African ancestors, Afro-Americans pass on much of their knowledge through folklore, music, proverbs, and religion. In addition, Afro-American culture, like African culture, tends to unite religion with all other aspects of life. Consequently, the church becomes a political, economic, and social center as well as a religious center for the black community.

Tracing ideology in oral cultures is a difficult but not impossible task. The most important point to keep in mind is that literacy and nonliteracy foster different modes of thinking. Writing spans space and time and makes possible phenomena like contracts and constitutions. It fosters precision, categorization, reflection, and detachment. However, orality should not be viewed as inferior to literacy. Nonliteracy avoids some of the problems of literacy, which can include rigidity, dogma, speciousness, and a lack of emotion and creativity. Oral thinking fosters the skills of performance, listening, and remembering. The limitations of orality are often offset by the use of proverbs, allegory, allusion, rite, music, dance, rhythm, sculpture, and art (Bozeman 1976, 70–74). Bozeman provides an example of nonliteracy and political organization:

> What the records of the most effective "greater societies" in pagan Africa illustrate is a marked ingenuity for rendering the principles of power, unity, and hierarchy by nonliterate means. An intricate order of superior and inferior stools can here take the place of a written federal constitution, even as each of these assembled objects, in its own right, communicates shared religious convictions and family tradition. And similar sacred and governmental functions are entrusted to drums, many of which are personalized, as it were, and endowed with intrinsic powers of their own. (Bozeman 1976, 138)

Bozeman is careful to remind us that while these institutions may be viewed as taking the place of certain Western institutions, they are in fact different and are perceived differently by Africans. In short, many Western concepts such as law, contract, and future stability have no traditional meaning in Africa.

While African orality is a dominant feature of Afro-American culture, its significance and functions have diminished as blacks have received formal education. Still, the pragmatism in the African worldview, which found its expression in African folklore and proverbs, survives today in the United States.

LANGUAGE AND CULTURAL DOMINANCE

The blues contains a number of excellent examples of the difficulties involved in searching for a black ideology. One of the difficulties is the use of "black English," which differs significantly from other varieties of English. According to linguist J. L. Dillard, the full scope of blues associations is not fully appreciated because "blues lyrics frequently contain 'hidden' meanings not perceived by the non-Black listener" (1977, 79). Other difficulties in analyzing blues concern superficial distinctions between "country" and "city," or "classic" blues and the view of blues as "evil" or "sad" music.

Even more difficult to trace than the "meaning of the blues" is the cultural significance of black speech. Yet linguistics represents one of the most highly developed scientific disciplines available for studying orality. Mervyn Alleyne describes these difficulties:

> Much more culturally significant than formal characteristics of Black speech may be the function attributed to language in Afro-American communities. This is because, whereas overt form can be relatively easily learned or diffused, function (as well as the underlying semantic content) belongs to a deep level of cultural behavior that is not easily subject to conscious tending. (Alleyne 1980, 9)

While Alleyne rejects the notion of a separate and homogeneous black urban community, he quotes approvingly Roger Abraham's conviction that the emotional behavior of black Philadelphians "may be characteristic of performances in most New World Negro Communities" (Abrahams in Alleyne 1980, 10).

The emphasis on lexicon rather than grammatical patterns in "black English" is not totally a product of accessibility. Ivan Van Sertima has charged:

> In the same way as the linguists sought to show that European elements had completely wiped out the African elements in the New World dialects—putting up a persuasive case by shifting focus from grammatical patterns to surface vocabulary—these folklorists are shifting focus from mythological structure to surface features of objects and incidents (motifs) to show that very little that is identifiably African survives in Afro-American folktales. (Van Sertima in Goldstein 1971, 26)

This tendency of some scholars to attribute certain characteristics of Afro-American speech and folktales to European roots has counterparts in music and religion. Various scholars have suggested that black spirituals are borrowed from white hymns, while ignoring the unique function of the spiritual in the black community (Lovell 1972). Similarly, the emotionalism of the black holiness and pentecostal groups has been traced to white evangelicals by some scholars (Myrdal 1948).

The role of culture in language development is important in the search for black political thought. If blacks are merely imitators rather than innovators, the possibility of a distinctive political ideology is bleak. Or, if their linguistic code is so limited as to prevent conceptualization, the prospects of maintaining any ideology are remote.[8] This latter position has been suggested by Claus Mueller (1973). He believes that the restricted speech code of the lower classes cannot be used in an instrumental, reflective way. The language of these individuals prevents them from transcending their social context and from relating to the larger society and its political institutions. It was not until the early sixties, says Mueller, that Afro-Americans were able to interpret symbolically their status in a political way on a widespread basis.

Mueller's analysis overlooks the efforts of several popular black leaders to communicate with a large audience prior to the sixties. Booker T. Washington established a network of newspapers, and Marcus Garvey published a news-paper with an international circulation. The real problem with Mueller's "liberal" interpretation of black status lies in its failure to distinguish between group identification and political consciousness. Of course, the upper classes can be more articulate than the lower classes, if we mean by articulate the power to shape and control modes of mass communication.

According to Murray Edelman, "public language"—which means shared norms and implicit understanding—"validates established beliefs and streng-thens the authority of the polity or organization in which it is used" (1977, 109). The use of certain highly developed terminologies and syntax that separate the observer and his premises from what he is studying gives the appearance of fact and objectivity. In a brilliant examination of the creation of the concept of "Orientalism," Edward Said states:

> Altogether an internally structural archive is built up from the literature that belongs to these experiences. Out of this comes a restricted number of typical encapsulations: the journey, the history, the fable, the stereotype, the polemi-cal confrontation. These are the lenses through which the Orient is ex-perienced, and they shape the language, perception, and form of the encoun-ter between East and West. (Said 1979, 58)

Said adds that "representations because they are embedded first in the lan-guage and then in the culture, institutions, and political ambience of the representer are something besides the 'truth,' which is itself a representation" (1979, 272). It is not the inability of the poverty-stricken in the East to articulate their own identities that creates Orientalism, because all classes are represented. Rather it is the power of the representer to control the mode of communication that distorts and stereotypes the represented. Herbert Blumer (1958) views such a process as racial prejudice based on a sense of group position rather a type of feeling lodged in individuals. It is just such a racial prejudice that some are arguing typified the mass media's coverage of Jesse Jackson's presidential campaigns (Broth 1987). In short, it is a collective process operating chiefly through the public media.

Of course, it is just such a process of cultural dominance through the media that Harold Cruse examines in his major work *The Crisis of the Negro In-tellectual.* Cruse sees a major value conflict in the idealization of individual rights on the one hand and the reality of a nation dominated by the social power of groups on the other. For Cruse, the intellectual is the only individual who can bridge such groups, and thus the Negro artist must serve as a spokesperson for blacks.

By focusing on the leadership of black intellectuals in general and creative artists in particular, Cruse may exacerbate black-white value conflicts. Most studies of elite ideology show a greater gap between the values of opposing leaders than among their respective followers. Therefore, the dilemma over integration versus segregation, which is central to Cruse's analysis, may have less meaning for black masses historically, because integration was not a viable option for most. Thus at the end of his analysis, Cruse is still left with a vital task: "The radical wing of the Negro movement in America sorely needs a social theory based on the living ingredients of Afro-American history" (1967, 557).

More recently, Rhett Jones has argued that the lack of an ideological structure which reflects the black experience in North America, just as the Enlightenment ideology developed by whites reflects their experience in the New World, is a central problem for all blacks, not merely for the radical wing (Jones 1988, 36). Such a theory or ideology must emerge naturally from the cultural history of a people. In short, it must be constructed from the ground up.

In the chapters that follow, we seek to examine cultural values of the black masses as they have emerged over time. To do this we must examine the oral tradition of the black community especially as manifested in the "blues" and in black folklore. These forms of mass communication are analyzed for their form or style of presentation as well as their content.

We also seek to explore the ways in which black cultural values have been incorporated and modified by black leaders and black institutions. By examining the style and substance of the messages of the most successful black leaders and black institutions, we can uncover the cultural frameworks or maps that have proven the most meaningful over time. Thus, the black church and its leadership are central subjects of our work.

Finally, we argue that there is a distinct black politics based on a unique style and combination of worldviews that informs black political behavior. This black politics contains the possibility of a synthesis between selfish individualism and group responsibility that could provide an instructive moral vision for the entire society.

CHAPTER
2
BLACK AND BLUE

I'm tired of this Jim Crow, gonna leave this Jim Crow town,

Doggone my black soul, I'm sweet Chicago bound,
Yes, I'm leavin' here, from this ole Jim Crow town,

I'm going up North, where they say—money grows on trees,
I don't give a doggone, if ma black soul leaves,
I'm goin' where I don't need no B.V.D.s.

I'm goin' up North, baby, I can't carry you,
Ain't nothin' in that cold country, a sweet gal can do,
I'm goin' get me another gal, baby, I'm through with you.

Lord well, if I get up there—where they don't suit—
I don't start no crying. Go tell that ole ma'am of mine,
Lord I'm ready to come back to my Jim Crow town.

—"Jim Crow Blues" Oliver

There is a pervasive pathology sweeping across our nation's suburbs and high rent districts. It is deeply rooted in our country's political and economic institutions and has been given new life by the Reagan administration. This tangle of deviant behavior and pathology may be termed the "culture of wealth."

Among the behavioral characteristics of groups succumbing to this culture are the following: First, a rejection or denial of their physical attributes. This rejection leads to hazardous sessions in tanning parlors or in extreme cases costly trips to tropical resorts in order to darken the skin. In addition, a major industry has sprung up in the field of weight-loss salons and diet books and doctors. No other group of people in the world is more concerned with *losing* weight than the "unworthy" rich. Second, members of this group exhibit a sense of rootlessness and an inability to make practical decisions. For example, many members of this group have homes in several locations, thus isolating themselves and hindering the development of lasting community contacts. They also isolate themselves in private social and dining clubs exhibiting extreme antisocial behavior. Most of the "undeserving" rich have several cars, many clothes, and art objects. In short, they demonstrate an inability to choose a single reliable vehicle, and they waste money on trendy fashions. Moreover, art objects have no practical use, although some of the enlightened rich use them as investments and store them in vaults. Finally, the culture of the rich is engulfed in a web of crime, sexism, and poor health. Drug use and white collar crime are rampant, according to every available index. Family structure invariably follows an outdated patriarchal model similar to the old "Ozzie and Harriet" or "Leave It to Beaver" television shows. Aside from weight problems, many of the rich are workaholics and suffer from an inability to relax. Ulcers, heart attacks, and gout are common ailments. In sum, this group is engaged in a permanent cycle of divorce, forced child separations through boarding schools, and rampant materialism that leads to the dreaded Monte Carlo syndrome. Before they can be helped they must close tax loopholes, end subsidies, and stop buying influence.

It seems odd that the deviant behavior of the wealthy has not spawned a literature devoted to analyzing their problems. Seldom are the rich referred to as "hard core" or "chronic" spenders. Nor are distinctions made between the deserving and the undeserving rich. Perhaps it is as Murray Edelman says, "Dominant categories of speech and of thought define the economically successful and the poltically powerful as meritorious, and the unsuccessful and politically deviant as mentally or morally inadequate" (Edelman 1977, 39). Yet it is clear that the behavior described above is not "normal" behavior in the sense that most Americans engage in it. It would also be difficult to attribute universal values to it since most inhabitants of this planet are more concerned with gaining weight than losing it.

Black conservative leaders promote this upper-class deviant culture, this possessive individualism as the norm. Yet the deviance of the wealthy from the middle-class norm is not seen as evidence of social pathology. Obviously, the differences between "high" culture and "low" culture reflect more than aesthetic taste. For if they did not, lower-class opera lovers would be proportionately as numerous as upper-class opera lovers, and the "pathologies" of the latter would receive as much attention as those of the former. After all, the themes of love, death, loneliness, and betrayal are as common in the opera as they are in country-and-western music or the blues. The "blues" people rather than the country-and-western devotees, however, have been singled out as deviant.

In fact, the culture-of-poverty concept moves away from the notion of black pathology to a position of lower-class pathology. There is an effort to demonstrate that deviant behavior is class-determined rather than racially determined. Such an argument make programs designed to assist the poor more feasible politically. Few if any efforts, however, are made to examine the deviant behavior of any ethnic group aside from blacks.[1] The characteristics of the culture of poverty, then, especially as they relate to government policy making have come to be almost exclusively associated with black culture. And black conservatives, as well as liberals and radicals, have often accepted the totally negative view of these characteristics. Yet by denying a group any culture, they are denied a basis of identity and the internal values needed to meaningfully interact with other groups and the larger society.

FOLK CULTURE AND BLACK TRADITIONALISM

There can be no doubt that the slave experience seriously weakened the African ontology. The classic debate launched by Melville Herskovits and E. Franklin Frazier over the question of African cultural survivals now usually takes the form of the extent to which the African worldview shaped Western practices, that is, the degree to which African form shaped Anglo-American content. It seems fairly certain that the most upwardly mobile elements of the slave and free black populations more readily shed themselves of African customs than those they left behind. In a sense, those who sought to please the master and to adopt the master's ways were profoundly conservative. They made a conscious choice as to their life style. In another sense, they were profoundly liberal to the extent that they harbored notions of equality, assimilation, and a possessive individualism.

By the same token the masses or peasants also reflected dual qualities. To the degree they attempted to maintain and preserve traditional African customs or worldviews they were conservative. On the other hand, the preservation of a distinct subculture with its own set of values represented a fundamental challenge to white cultural dominance. It provided the basis for both conservative black nationalism and radical black nationalism. Perhaps this is why black conservatives and nationalists often sound alike in their emphasis on self-esteem and achievement, as Bernard Boxill contends (1984, 51). At this point, Karl Mannheim's distinction between "traditionalism" as the emotional and relatively inarticulate tendency to hold on to established and inherited patterns of life and "conservatism" which is "conscious and reflective from the first, since it arises as a counter movement in conscious opposition to the highly organized, coherent, and systematic 'progressive' movement" is instructive (Mannheim quoted in Fredrickson, 48).[2] Using the terminology of contemporary social science, one might say that traditionalism is the expression of group identification while conservatism represents the political consciousness of a group. However, group identification can serve as a basis for radical as well as conservative political consciousness.

A major example of Afro-American traditionalism is found in black folklore. Ralph Ellison, both a liberal and a conservative writer, has said:

> . . . folklore offers the first drawings of any group's character. It preserves mainly those situations which have repeated themselves again and again in the history of any given group. It describes those rites, manners, customs, and so forth, which insure the good life, or destroy it; and it describes those boundaries of feeling, thought, and action which that particular group has found to be the limitation of the human condition. It projects this wisdom in symbols which express the group's will to survive; it embodies those values by which the group lives and dies. These drawings may be crude but they are nonetheless profound in that they represent the group's attempt to humanize the world. . . . (1964, 172).

Examples of this folk wisdom have been found by Mary Berry and John Blassingame in at least 122 West African proverbs directly imported by the slaves. The slaves borrowed less than 20 percent of their proverbs from their white masters. In addition to those slave proverbs and their West African parallels listed by Berry and Blassingame, we have collected several more which share a common theme.

These African and Afro-American proverbs, as well as many not listed, cover a broad spectrum of daily situations ranging from the mundane to life-threatening. Some reflect philosophical concerns such as death, true friendship, aging, and inequality. Many are conservative in their call for patience and respect for authority, while some indicate that the wealthy and powerful can overstep their bounds and become too greedy. These proverbs do not constitute an ideology in the Western sense, but they do comprise a worldview along with a mechanism of socialization.

Like the proverb, the folktale served some of the same functions in America as it had in Africa. Among them were inculcating morality in the young, teaching the value of cooperation, explaining animal behavior, and providing amusement. Yet the situation of the slave was not comparable to the African environment, and folklore had unique functions among Afro-Americans. The use of cunning to overcome strength as in Br'er Rabbit, hiding anger behind a mask of humility as did Uncle Remus, laughing in the face of adversity as did the "Bad Nigger," creating heroes like John Henry, violating plantation rules in the manner of High John de Conquer, and retaining hope in spite of the odds as in the development of disaster songs; these customs point to values and norms worth preserving and in fact necessary for survival. Whereas the traditionalism of African culture might remain unchallenged and unconscious, the traditionalism of Afro-American culture was challenged and for some became conscious. It retains the useful while dropping the irrelevant. It becomes pragmatic, flexible and dual-edged.[3]

TABLE 1

Slave Proverbs and Their African Parallels

Slave proverb	African parallel	Theme/explanation
If you play with a puppy, he will lick your face.[a]	If you play with a dog, you must expect it to lick your mouth. (Ashanti)	Familiarity with inferiors may cause them to lose respect for you
Distant stovewood is good stovewood.	Distant firewood is good firewood. (Ewe)	Things look better from a distance
"Almost kill bird" don't make soup.	"I nearly killed the bird." No one can eat "nearly" in a stew. (Yoruba) "Almost" is not eaten. (Zulu)	(Literal)
One rain won't make a crop.	One tree does not make a forest. (Ewe, Kpelle, Ashanti)	One part does not equal the whole
The pitcher goes to the well every day; one day it will leave its handle.	If there is a continual going to the well, one day there will be a smashing of the pitcher. (Hausa)	One's evil deeds will one day be discovered
A seldom visitor makes a good friend.	If you visit your fellow (friend) too often, he will not respect you. But if you make yourself scarce, he will pine for your company. (Jabo)	(Literal)
A scornful dog will eat dirty pudding.	When a dog is hungry, it eats mud. (Zulu)	Adversity causes one to do things he would not do in good times
He holds with the hare (or fox) and runs with the hounds.	They forbid ram and eat sheep. (Ibo)	A deceitful person
The best swimmer is often drowned.	The expert swimmer is carried away by the water. (Zulu, Tonga)	There is no absolute certainty of anything
Tater-vine growin' while you sleep.[b]	Sleep is the cousin of death. (Congo)	Laziness
Sleepin' in de fence-corner don't fetch Christmas in de kitchen.	The man on his feet carries off the share of the man sitting down. (Guinea)	Laziness

You can hide de fire, but w'at you gwine do wid de smoke?	If you are hiding, don't light a fire. (Ashanti) If you burn a house, can you conceal the smoke? (Ashanti)	Consequences
Licker talks mightly loud w'en it git loose fum de jug.	When the cock is drunk, he forgets about the hawk. (Ashanti)	Drunkeness
Tarrypin walk fast 'nuff fer to go visitin'!	The moon moves slowly, but it crosses town. (Ashanti)	Patience
Troubles is seasonin! Simmons ain't good til dey'er fros'-bit.	The flesh of a young animal tastes flat. (Congo) Man is like palm-wine: when young, sweet but without strength, in old age, strong but harsh. (Congo)	Virtues of old age
Rain-crow don't sing no chune, but you can 'pend on 'im.	The heart of the wise man lies quiet like limpid water. (Cameroon)	Virtues of calmness
Better de gravy dan no grease 'tall.	Little is better than nothing. (Nigeria) Better rotten teeth than empty mouth. (Hausa)	Appreciation
(It) don't rain eve'y time de pig squeal	Thunder is not yet rain. (Kenya)	Over-expectation
Rooster makes mo' racket dan de hen w'at lay de aig.	He who boasts much can do little. (Niger)	Bragging
Neber 'sprise a bridge dat carries you safely ober.	Do not call the forest that shelters you a jungle. (Ashanti) Do not tell the man who is carrying you that he stinks. (Sierre Leone)	Gratitude

[a]This and the following eight proverbs were collected by Berry and Blassingame in *Long Memory* (p. 21).
[b]This and the following proverbs were collected by me.

It is in the pioneering work of Sterling Stuckey (1968), John Blassingame (1972), and particularly Lawrence Levine (1977) that we see the direct link between Afro-American folklore and worldview. Levine, like some scholars before him, attributes both this-worldly and other-worldly functions to the spirituals. By publicly stating their worth, often as "chosen people," they helped slaves fight the stereotyped images of them as inferior. Like John Lovell, Sterling Brown, and others, Levine indicates that the spirituals were also used to convey this-world messages of escape and rebellion. However, Levine goes on to contrast the sacred worldview of the spirituals with the more mundane and secular world of folklore and especially trickster tales. In these tales, the weak used their wits to confront and evade the strong. The prizes to be won—in contrast to salvation or freedom as offered by the spiritual—included not only self-preservation but wealth, success, prestige, honor, and sexual prowess. In the trickster tales, ambition to gain these rewards and the amoral manipulation of other animals was ubiquitous. Both the spirituals and the animal tales had African roots. They also provided group solidarity and proper socialization. *Yet their functions in the slave world were divergent.* The spirituals provided a universal moral framework of historic proportions, while the animal tales were personal guides to daily survival.

John W. Roberts has argued that the contradictions between the amorality of the trickster tales and the morality of the spirituals have been overlooked because folklorists tend to concentrate on a single genre rather than on the development of certain ideas within the folk tradition of a single folk group. He contends that in comparing the two, the trickster tales do not offer a moral basis for criticizing slavery or for conceptualizing action to bring about its collapse, whereas these elements are clearly a part of the spiritual's worldview. In this sense, the trickster tales may be seen as a passive and conservative strategy that promotes a vision of the world which could be seen as a valida-tion of slavery—a giant trick. "Furthermore," says Roberts, "unlike the trickster of other cultural groups, especially Native American, the Afro-American trick-ster has no association with religion which in many ways makes him a unique figure from this perspective" (Roberts 1982, 104).

Roberts apparently missed E. C. L. Adams's collection of Afro-American folktales from the Congaree swamps of South Carolina. In "Bur Rabbit in Red Hill Churchyard" we see the trickster as a musician with a religious function. He fiddles a man up out of his grave, has a conversation with him, and returns him to the grave: "After dey done wored dey self out wid compersation, I see Bur Rabbit take he fiddle an' put it under he chin an' start to playin'. An' while I watch, I see Bur Rabbit step back on de grave an' Simon were gone" (Adams 1928, 173). In this case, the trickster represents a much more traditional religious alternative related to magic and witchcraft than the spirituals, which combine New World Christianity with traditional values.

While the heroic world of Moses as embodied in the spirituals provides a sharp contrast to the Br'er Rabbit of the "Tar Baby" tale, one cannot lose sight of the important psychological and even physical contributions the trickster tales provided the slave community. Still, if one is to construct an Afro-American ideology, a stronger rock is found in the spirituals—as evidenced during the civil rights movement—than in the individualistic, manipulative and often exploitative world of the trickster. Both traditions belong to the slave community and are not a function of class but rather of need.

POST–CIVIL WAR CULTURE

The impact of the Civil War and the abolition of slavery are reflected both in Afro-American culture and in politics. The oneness and yearning for freedom that marked the rise of the spiritual were created by the institution of slavery. With its abolition, the freed Negro had new opportunities to explore the white world beyond the plantation. The ex-slave was no longer forced to remain in one place with one people. During "radical" Reconstruction integration proceeded with varying degrees of success along various fronts. As individualism and the development of industrial capitalism gripped the nation, it also took hold of the black imagination. The sacred worldview of historic dimensions was replaced by a more pragmatic secular outlook concerned with material acquisition and upward mobility.

The central position accorded the "sacred world" of slave folk culture by Levine has been challenged by V. P. Franklin. He contends that Levine ignored a flourishing secular folk culture that developed outside the purview of whites. These songs and tales reinforced the values of resistance against unjust oppression, which was the common denominator of all slaves. Thus, says Franklin, racial oppression, not religion, occupied the central position in defining the emerging value system of the Afro-American masses (1984, 145).

Since racial oppression did not cease with the coming of emancipation, Franklin contends that there was no significant change in the predominant cultural values and attitudes within the black community. In his terms, there was a profound legal change in the status of Afro-Americans, but their fundamental material conditions remained the same. This view contrasts sharply with Levine's position that "freedom" or emancipation transformed Afro-American folk culture from a religious to a more secular orientation.

We agree with Franklin that there was great continuity in Afro-American cultural values from slavery to freedom. Under slavery, says Franklin, blacks valued survival with dignity, resistance against oppression, religious self-determination, and freedom. He argues that they continued to hold these ideals after emancipation, with freedom, rather than being an end in itself, becoming a means for achieving other cultural goals.

While we agree with Franklin that the values of resistance against oppression and religious self-determination remained a vital part of black folk culture, it is impossible to conclude that the profound change in black political and legal status had no cultural impact. Material conditions notwithstanding, freedom as a means presented new options and alternatives. The value system of whites now became a real possibility within the black worldview. These options, in turn, created the basis for increased intraracial value conflict. The content of the antebellum value system was expanded, but most importantly the form of expression or communication of these values changed.

This modified worldview was expressed in the rise of the secular leadership of Booker T. Washington as well as in Afro-American folk culture. Lawrence Levine states that "there was a direct relationship between the national ideological emphasis upon the individual, the popularity of Booker T. Washington's teachings, and the rise of the blues" (1977, 223). This new psychological, social, and economical acculturation would have been impossible during slavery and was reflected in sacred music as well as secular music.

Did this acculturation mean that blacks had totally adopted the Horatio Alger model and abandoned their sense of communality?

> The rise of the blues embodies much of the complexity for the cultural historian that the rise of gospel music does. Gospel song was a musical and structural return to African and slave music and away from Western hymnology, even while its lyrics—its message—evidenced an abandonment of the sacred universe of the African and slave past and an adjustment to modern religious consciousness. The development of blues poses some of these same paradoxes. The personalized, solo elements of the blues style may indicate a decisive move into twentieth century American consciousness, but the musical style of the blues indicates a holding on to the old roots at the very time when the dispersion of Negroes throughout the country and the rise of the radio and phonograph could have spelled the demise of a distinctive Afro-American musical style . . . blues with its emphasis upon improvisation, its retention of call and response pattern, its polyrhythmic effects, and its methods of vocal production which included slides, slurs, vocal leaps, and the use of falsetto, was a definite assertion of central elements of the traditional communal musical style. (Levine 1977, 223–24)

In other words, at a time when blacks question the sacred worldview and consciously adopt the rampant economic liberalism (individualism) of the day, they nonetheless reject white culture or "white style" and return, perhaps unconsciously, to traditional roots.

Again in *Black Culture and Black Consciousness*, Lawrence Levine states that "[f]reedom ultimately weakened the cultural self-containment characteristic of the slaves and placed an increasing number of Negroes in a culturally marginal situation" (Levine 1977, 138). Blacks were now poised between two cultures: one held security and black tradition, the other offered the promise of upward mobility. As the sacred worldview of the spirituals lost its functional importance after emancipation and urbanization created new social problems, two new musical forms arose to replace it. One form was gospel music and the other was the blues. And while it is sometimes difficult to distinguish between the two, particularly with a song like "When the Saints Come Marching In," we will contend that these two forms represent significantly different ways of confronting life. They are different stylistic strategies. Moreover, we will contend that gospel music, despite its African traits, is more assimilative in character and other-worldly in strategy.[4] Blues on the other hand, represents a more this-worldly orientation with an attitude that challenges divine power and goodness.

Religious affiliation has been directly linked to the style of musical performance. Negro Presbyterian, Congregational, and Episcopalian churches were made up largely of middle- and upper-class blacks, and the congregation or choir sang either "cooly" standard hymns or selected spirituals or "anthems."[5] Larger Baptist and Methodist churches often featured two choirs; one sang Euro-American hymns, and the other sang black gospel songs. In the storefront Baptist and Methodist churches and in the Holiness and Spiritualist churches, spirituals, gospel songs, and old hymns were enthusiastically sung by the entire congregation. These services were attended by lower-class blacks and denigrated as too emotional and wild by the middle class (Levine 1977, 188).

The development of the gospel song, particularly in the churches of the lower and lower-middle classes, symbolized a move toward assimilation despite the objections of those who were better off.[6] In its solo style with other-worldly themes, the gospel was closer in form and content to Euro-American religious music than the spiritual. The attitudes of many churchgoers to the old secular slave songs also represented a break with tradition. Many were ashamed of the old "sinful" songs and refused to sing them. The developing blues was also attacked as "devil music." Yet Levine states that "[b]lues was threatening because its spokesmen and its ritual too frequently provided the expressive communal channels of relief that had been largely the province of religion in the past" (ibid., 237). The blues, then, successfully blended the sacred and secular, while gospel did not.

In light of the criticism of the blues by black churchgoers, it may seem strange to indicate that it has a sacred component. Paul Garon believes that it is "uncompromisingly atheistic: The blues do not intervene on the theological plane with the obsolete tools of rationalism or in the name of some empty 'humanism.' On the contrary, it enters the fray wholeheartedly *on the side of Evil*" (Garon 1979, 136, emphasis mine). It would appear that Garon has mistaken theology for rationalism. While the blues is not theological, it is certainly rational. Garon also mistakes blues' references to voodoo and conjure as evil.

The many blues songs involving "black magic" or "conjure" represent a deeper level of black religion than even the "sanctified" church. Conjure or Hoo doo represents African religion, not atheism. Robert Johnson's "Hell-bound on My Trail" is an example:

You sprinkled hot foot powder umm around my door,
all around my door,
It keeps me with a rambling mind, rider, every old
place I go,
every old place I go.

I've got to keep moving, I've got to keep moving,
Blues falling down like hail, blues falling down like hail.

(Dillard 1977, 75)

Many blues musicians or composers, like Thomas Dorsey, Blind Lemon Jefferson, Joe Turner, Big Bill Broonzy, Bessie Smith, and Jelly Roll Morton, had been or continued to be deeply religious. Dorsey composed blues before he "invented" the gospel song. Morton was a devout Catholic who could not entirely escape voodoo. Bessie Smith tried to get to church every Sunday even when on the road and often sang hymns around the house when not traveling (Oakley 1977, 116). J. L. Dillard attributes a large part of the "sinful" or "evil" reputation of the blues to "its association with the behavior pattern of conjure" (ibid., 82).

It is our contention that the failure of the gospel song to deal with this world, along with the harsh conditions facing blacks in the post–Reconstruction South, provides ample material for an alternative worldview that was the blues. This worldview had its roots in African religion and secular slave songs. James Cone reports that this evidence of open rebellion against God in the blues also implies a stubborn "refusal to go beyond the existential problem and substitute other-worldly answers" (Cone 1972, 110). For the less rebellious, this questioning of God is reflected in the development of religious disaster songs which exhibit a more strident, less secure effort to prove God's existence in tragedies (Levine 1977, 174).

Benjamin Mays has said "that the Negro's idea of God grows out of his social situation. The cosmological and teleological conceptions of God are conspicuous by their absence in Negro literature" (Mays 1968, 254). Mays believed that the social, educational, and economic upheaval resulting from World War I and its aftermath had produced an upheaval in the thinking of the elite with respect to God, but not among the masses.[7] Mays, however, confined his analysis to the music and sermons of the black church. Had he examined the blues, he would have found that the black masses were also questioning the idea of God. However, it was the Christian concept of God that was questioned as well as the hypocrisy of the Christians.

THE "BLUES" CULTURE

The question remains as to whether the worldview represented by the blues or blues culture is capable of providing the values and social vision necessary to construct an ideology. In short, is it merely a mechanism or style of survival like the trickster tales, or does it constitute the basis of a new moral order?

A number of scholars including Oscar Lewis, Lee Rainwater, Herbert J. Gans, Hyman Rodman, Elliot Liebow, and others believe that most of the poor share the values and aspirations of the working and middle classes. The divergence between their aspirations and their behavior is a function of their poverty. In terms of pathology, most view the behavior of the poor as realistic responses to a particular situation. The type of response may vary according to the individual. However, alternative norms are often developed to explain failure and provide support among peers.

Ulf Hannerz has identified the major construction materials of the ghetto-specified male alternative as norms which are actually supported by mainstream culture. These include strong, overt concerns with sexual exploitation, toughness and ability to command respect, personal appearance with an emphasis on male clothing fashions, liquor consumption, and verbal ability (Hannerz 1969, 79). It is important to note that Hannerz does not identify all ghetto males as supporting these norms. He indicates that "swingers" and "streetcorner men" are more attracted to such normative models than "mainstreamers." In addition, Hannerz states that "[n]o ghetto-specific model for a male-female union has anything close to the normative validity which the mainstream model enjoys in the ghetto as well as outside it, and this makes it hard for couples to find a state of union which is as morally satisfying to them" (ibid., 102).

In his *Urban Blues*, Charles Keil attempts to identify some of the positive and unique elements of Negro culture in contrast to the negative images of the culture of poverty theorists. Keil believes that "the hustler and the entertainer are ideal types representing two important value orientations for the lower class Negro" and must not be viewed as deviants or shadow figures (Keil 1966, 20). In fact, says Keil, a good preacher can be viewed as both a hustler and an entertainer. In comparing Martin Luther King's preaching to that of B. B. King, he argues that blues singing is more a priestly role than an artistic one (i.e., it is ritualistic). However, the bluesman's politics and preaching are always related to families.

By focusing on sexual themes in the blues, Keil challenges the view that lower-class Negro life styles are products of overcompensation for masculine self-doubt:

> To begin with, it is entirely possible that "the Oedipal problem of managing and diverting aggression against the father may be easily resolved, mitigated or avoided altogether in families in which the father is absent or weak and where a number of mothering women are in or near the household. (Ibid., 23)

> The battle of the sexes can of course be found raging in many slums around the world—for example, Athens, Mexico City, Liverpool, Johannesburg—but in most of these "cultures of poverty" the battle tends to be resolved in terms of male authoritarianism rather than "mother-centeredness." (Ibid., 10)

While Keil defends black lower-class styles, his essential view still accepts many of the characteristics outlined by poverty-culture theorists. Despite his defense of Negro culture, his solutions to the problems facing urban blacks include programs such as Operation Headstart. He adds that the blues will not disappear with integration, because they are centered primarily on sexual conflict rather than racial conflict (ibid., 99). And apparently he assumes that sexual conflict is cultural rather than situational.

Michael Haralambos appears to contradict Keil's argument in an indirect though concrete way. He contends that the decline of the blues in the sixties "is primarily a function of the decline of Jim Crow to which the music, and the attributes and strategies is presented, was adapted" (Haralambos 1974, 151). Neither unemployment rates nor relative income correlate with the production of blues records. In fact, the success of the civil rights movement and the rise of black pride, says Haralambos, account for decreasing black interest in the blues. It was soul music that rose to meet new black attitudes in the sixties.

As it relates to sexual relationships, however, soul music and the new black pride form a more complicated phenomenon. Haralambos admits that the percentage of black female-headed households and the rate of divorce among blacks continued to rise during the sixties. However, he claims that soul music themes express "a determination to maintain and improve relationships, an advocacy of standard marital roles as the ideal and a celebration of their successful translation into action and a general perspective of hope and optimism in regard to relations between men and women."[8]

If the decline of the blues and the rise of soul music mark a profound shift in the outlook of black Americans, as Haralambos and Giles Oakley contend, it is a shift reflected in the style of presentation rather than in economic or sexual indicators. Such a shift resembles the transition from spirituals to gospel music that occurred after the Civil War. Haralambos and Oakley overstate the passivity and resignation of the blues, just as they overstate the optimism of sixties soul music which has its roots in the blues. Oakley's own work cites Bessie Smith as an extraordinary and powerful spirit. In her "Young Woman's Blues" (1926) she sings:

> I'm a young woman an' ain't done runnin' round,
> Some people call me a hobo, some call me a bum,
> Nobody knows my name, nobody knows what I've done,
> I'm as good as any woman in your town.
> I ain't high yellow, I'm deep yellow-brown,
> I ain't goin' to marry, ain't goin' to settle down,
> I goin' drink good moonshine an' run these brown down,
> See that long lonesome road—don't you know its gotta end,
> An' I'm a good woman an' I can get plenty men.

(Oakley 1977, 111)

TABLE 2

Unemployment Rates, Relative Income, Blues Records

Year	Non-white unemployment rate	Non-white relative income	Number of blues records
1950	9.0	54	270
1951	5.3	53	310
1952	5.4	57	270
1953	4.5	56	220
1954	9.9	56	230
1955	8.7	55	150
1956	8.3	53	120
1957	7.9	54	160
1958	12.6	51	100
1959	10.7	52	110
1960	10.2	55	140
1961	12.4	53	140
1962	10.9	53	110
1963	10.8	53	70
1964	9.6	56	80
1965	8.1	55	80
1966	7.3	60	90

The unemployment rate is the percentage of unemployment in the civilian labor force. Relative income is the median income of non-white families as a percentage of white family income. Source: Haralambos

Bessie Smith's blues strike an aggressive, optimistic, race conscious, independent chord not readily matched by the Supremes.

Bessie Smith is just the best known of many female blues singers who sought a direct identification with the black women in the audience. Carl Van Vechten reported the near hysteria and semireligious frenzy caused when Bessie proclaimed to a 1925 Orpheum Theatre crowd that "It's true I loves you, but I won't take mistreatment any mo'," and a girl sitting beneath his box called "Dat's right! Say it, Sister" (Van Vechten quoted in ibid., 117).

THE BLUES AS PROTEST

Although the explicit protest of singers like Bessie Smith may be unusual, less explicit protest may be hidden or implied during performance. The very survival of certain themes and styles is an indication of their universality. John Lovell agrees with Alan Marriam that song texts are not only an expression of deep-seated values but also an expression of thoughts and ideas not permissibly verbalized in other (both inter- and intra-racial) contexts (Lovell 1972,

8–9). And Alan Lomax adds that "[s]ince a folksong is transmitted orally by all or most means of a culture, generation after generation, it represents an extremely high consensus about patterns of meaning and behavior of cultural rather than individual significance" (ibid., 9). It should also reflect changes in that consensus as various themes or song types decline in popularity.

LeRoi Jones (Imamu Amiri Baraka) has taken just such an approach in *Blues People*. He believes that it might be possible to chart Negro social history through the frequency of reference to certain song types. One could "pretty well determine his social, economic, and psychological states at that particular period" (Jones 1963, 65). Frank Kofsky has contended that it is political ideology, specifically black nationalism, that has influenced the "timing and direction of stylistic innovations." Moreover, he argues that jazz musicians have been "the first to be converted and to espouse the tenets of black nationalism" (Kofsky 1970, 27).

In their books, Jones and Kofsky are concerned with demonstrating social and political change as reflected in the styles of blues musicians. Jones believes that blues and "real-jazz" (blues-derived jazz) are lower-class phenomena representing the only Negro music free of white dilutions. He is concerned, then, that when blues moves from a functional, folk music to an entertainment music played by professionals, it attains universality but loses some of its meaning for Negroes. In doing so it also reflects the continuing social mobility of Negroes as a group. For example, says Jones, the influx of Negroes into high schools and colleges by the late twenties was bound to leave traces. According to Jones, "[t]he most expressive big bands of the late twenties and thirties were largely middle-class Negro enterprises." Professionals went into jazz "to make money" and musicians/composers like Duke Ellington "used musical materials that were familiar to concert-trained ears" (Jones 1963, 160–62).

Kofsky's *Black Nationalism and the Revolution in Music* elaborates on Jones's political theme. Specifically, he argues that the development of bebop was an attempt to devise a music that whites could not play, thus rescuing black music from swing musicians like Benny Goodman and Paul Whiteman. The white reaction, aided by the record industry created during World War II, was "cool jazz" which not coincidently emerged during the early Cold War period. The black response to "cool jazz," says Kofsky, was the development of hard bop which reflected the civil rights and African liberation movements (Kofsky 1970, 32–49). Jones adds that the "step from *cool* to *soul* is a form of social aggression" that attempts to redefine the white canons of values (Jones 1963, 219). Thus, Jones and Kofsky attempt to identify an indigenous black nationalism in blues/jazz and examine the changes that occur with commercialization and professionalization.

Other blues scholars have sought to link the blues with social protest. In *Blues & the Poetic Spirit*, Paul Garon declares that the blues is clearly rebellious and revolutionary. However, as a surrealist, Garon is more interested in the poetry of the blues as it reflects sexual freedom than he is with explicit political protest. According to Garon the revolutionary nature of the blues lies in "its fidelity to fantasy and desire" which "generates an irreducible and, so to speak habit forming demand for freedom and . . . 'true life' " (Garon 1979, 64). In short, Garon sees the blues as a challenge to the moral norms and hypocrisy of American culture.

The lyrics of some blues songs are explicitly political. They might be entirely class-oriented like "Don't Take Away My P.W.A."

> Lord, Mister President, listen to what I'm
> going to say, [twice]
> You can take away all of the alphabet but
> please leave the P.W.A. [Public Work's Administration]
>
> Now you're in Mister President, an' I hope
> you're there to stay [twice]
> But whatever changes you make, please keep the P.W.A.
> P.W.A. is the best ol' friend I even seen, [twice]
> Since the job ain't hard, and the boss ain't mean.
>
> I went to the poll and voted, an' I know I
> voted the right way, [twice]
> Now I'm praying to you Mister President,
> Please keep the P.W.A.
>
> (Oliver 1960, 60)

Other themes take a more nationalistic (and utopian) line:

> Well, I'm going' to buy me a little
> railroad of my own,
> Ain't goin' to let nobody ride but de chocolate to the
> bone.
>
> (Dundes 1973, 495)

More common are themes that combine race and class, such as Big Bill Broonzy's *Black, Brown and White:*

> I went to an employment office
> Got a number and I got in line
> They called everybody's number
> But they never did call mine.
>
> They say if you's white, should be all right
> If you's brown, stick around
> But as you're black
> Mmm, Mmm, Brother, git back, git back, git back.
>
> (Levine 1977, 252)

Huddie Ledbetter's "Bourgeois Blues" is another example:

> Me and my wife run all over town,
> Everywhere we'd go people would run us down.
>
> [Refrain]
>
> Lawd, in the bourgeois town, ooh the bourgeois town,
> I got the bourgeois blues, gonna spread the news aroun
>
> Me and Marthy we was standin' upstairs,
> Heard a White man say, "I don't want no niggers up
> there."
>
> Me and my wife we went all over town,
> Everywhere we go the coloured people turn us down.
>
> White folks in Washington, they know how—
> Chuck a coloured man a nickel just to see him bow.
>
> Tell all the coloured folks t' listen to me,
> Don't try to buy no home in Washington D.C.

> (Oliver 1960, 209–10)

Compared to the frequency of themes like male-female relations and travel (especially railroads), the number of explicitly political protest-oriented blues is small. Oliver attributes their relative scarcity to the "Negro's acceptance of the stereotypes that have been cut for him" (ibid., 322). To accept Oliver's explanation one has to ignore other musical forms such as work songs and prison songs, which are often protest-oriented (see Jackson 1974a). More importantly, however, Oliver misses two essential characteristics of the blues: its function as a technique of survival or attitude toward life, and its function as a channel of intraracial communication and conflict resolution. In the performance of a song like "Bourgeois Blues" both functions are fulfilled.

Oliver's work on the blues has also been criticized as melodramatic sociology. Stanley Edgar Hyman believed Oliver lacked an understanding of "the private language of the blues, the sexual double-talk, and that what he takes to be sociology is almost always sexuality." This leads Oliver to mistake songs like "Cotton Picking Blues" as worker lamentations rather than a complaint concerning sexual infidelity. Hyman prefers to view the blues as complex, ironic, and sophisticated art rather than social protest. "They are," says Hyman, "not the disease but the doctor" (Hyman 1978, 174).

Building on Hyman's work, Ralph Ellison has challenged LeRoi Jones's "attempts to impose an ideology" upon the cultural complexity of the blues (Ellison 1966, 249). He argues that Negro musicians have never, as a group, felt alienated from any music sounded within their hearing and that Negro audiences have never been rigidly divided in terms of color, education, and income. Yet, in an earlier essay in the same volume, Ellison echoes Jones's separatism in his discussion of Charlie Christian's background. Ellison states that

> jazz was regarded by most of the respectable Negroes of the town Oklahoma City as a backward, low-class form of expression, and there was a marked difference between those who accepted and lived close to their folk experience and those whose status strivings led them to reject and deny it. (Ibid., 232–33)

Thus, on the one hand, Ellison can criticize Jones for viewing bop as a conscious gesture of separatism, while on the other hand he states that among the younger musicians of the thirties the "desire to master the classical technique was linked with the struggle for recognition in the larger society, and with a desire to throw off those non-musical features which came into Jazz from the minstrel tradition" (ibid., 233). The mastery of technique, then, is not solely related to aesthetics. Jones and Ellison really disagree about the politics of the bop artists and not about their music as such.

A parallel movement occurs among black poets from Phyllis Wheatley to those of the Harlem Renaissance. Their chief concern was to demonstrate their ability to write as well as whites. This period produced both dialect poets and those seeking to avoid any overt racial considerations. According to Stephen Henderson, the poetry of the twenties helped to balance the pieties of the abolitionist writers on the one hand and the bucolic idylls of the dialect school on the other, by offering the first realistic view of Afro-Americans in both their successes and their failures. By contrast, says Henderson, the black poetry movement of the sixties differs from "the Harlem Renaissance in the extent of its attempt to speak directly to Black people about themselves in order to move them toward self-knowledge and collective freedom. It is therefore not 'protest' art but essentially art of liberating vision" (Henderson 1973, 16). The Harlem Renaissance, then, represents black group identification, whereas the sixties reflect a more sophisticated black political consciousness.

In part Jones's political extrapolations fail because he attempts to impose an ideology on the black musician rather than draw one from him or her. This leads Jones to see the artist as a passive receptor of outside influences rather than a creative force. Such a position enables Jones to make a distinction between classic blues as entertainment and country blues as folklore, a position which Ellison rightly attacks. Ellison believes that, depending on the time and function, the blues may have either quality. For the larger society Bessie Smith may have been a "blues Queen," but within the tighter Negro community, "she was a priestess, a celebrant who affirmed the blues of the group and man's ability to deal with chaos" (ibid., 249–50).

Ellison demonstrates his concern for the creative freedom of the artist in his classic *Invisible Man.* As Ellison's narrator comments on his desire to hear five recordings of Louis Armstrong playing and singing "What Did I Do to Be So Black and Blue"—all at the same time—Ellison links the jazz style with a blues rendition in a meaningful way. According to Gene Bluestein, Ellison knows that Armstrong plays cornet (later trumpet) and that this instrument is associated with military bands. The marching band was one of the musical traditions absorbed and adapted by early New Orleans jazz groups. Bluestein states that what Armstrong does with the military tradition is related to what he makes of his invisibility: he blends the inflexible lockstep militarism into a lyrical sound as he turns the condition of invisibility into poetry (Bluestein 1972, 134). "It is an affirmation of the ability to overcome oppression through the creation of art," says Bluestein, "and it is another example of Ellison's tendency to associate the idea of freedom with the awareness of form" (ibid., 134).

In a more positive sense, Armstrong and the jazz he represents create a new sense of time. Instead of the regular precision of a military march rhythm there is the offbeat of the jazz style. Yet Armstrong, unlike Ellison's narrator, is not aware of his invisibility, because he is positively and deeply associated with the cultural sources of his art. The jazz musician's individual performance also demands allegiance to the group (ibid., 134–35). In short, Armstrong's traditionalism provides the basis for a new dynamic synthesis, while Ellison's terribly conscious and isolated narrator sits immobile and invisible.

THE BLUES AS ART

Black music in general and the blues and spirituals in particular have been cited by many as America's most original contribution to world culture. While there has been some controversy over the origins of Negro spirituals (see Lovell 1972), it is certain that Afro-Americans adapted them to their own style of worship. There is no doubt about the origin of the blues. While it is not certain when and where it arose, it is clear that it is the product of a number of Afro-American musical traditions including spirituals, the ring shout, work songs, hollers, prison songs, and ballads. As Dena Epstein indicates "[s]ecular music flourished among the exiled Africans to a much greater degree than had been recognized" (Epstein 1977, 345). There were many specialized songs that accompanied tasks like rowing, corn husking, cotton picking, street vending, grinding, spinning, and viewing. Rising up during the last quarter of the nineteenth century the blues' African roots are reflected in collective participation, antiphony, polyphony, heightened rhythm, talking instruments, slurs, falsetto singing, and "blues" notes (Chernoff 1979; Southern 1971; Jones 1963; Murray 1976).

The African influence on the blues is also reflected in its function. African music is relied on to maintain happiness and community spirit. Its functions include the control of bad persons and the praising of good ones; the recitation of history, poetry, and proverbs; the celebration of funerals and festivals, competition and games, religious worship, and socialization (Chernoff 1979, 167). Among the Fon of Dahomey there is a song for the loss of one's first tooth. The Akan of Ghana have a song for bed-wetters, while the Bamoun of the Cameroons have one for hanging court officials (Roberts 1972, 5). The diversity of song types is almost as great in the Afro-American tradition. And Paul Oliver argues that the blues encompasses more topics than any other known folk type.

In Africa it is difficult to distinguish between the traditional arts. A ritual using masked dancers might involve a dance performance, drama, a musical performance, poetry, the use of art objects (masks), and religious worship (Chernoff 1979, 34). Albert Murray relates this use of art in Africa to Afro-America through the blues. He believes that blues is first and foremost dance music. As such it serves the purpose of involving the entire community in participation (ritual courtship). Those black musicians who become more interested in technique than dance or in playing for other musicians or in concert halls are missing the point. Anyway, says Murray, "the quality of dance music may actually be of far greater significance than that of concert music. . . . Dance, after all, not only antedates music, but is also probably the most specific source of music and most of the other art forms as well" (Murray 1976, 189).

In *The Omni-Americans* Murray criticized Kenneth Clark's *Dark Ghetto* for indicting Negroes for having a low suicide rate. Moreover, Clark "confuses the personal motives of homicide with the socialized motives leading to welfare" (Murray 1971, 67). It is just such thinking that leads some to dismiss the blues as all complaint and misery—a veritable tangle of immorality, vice, and violence. Aside from the omission of many blues tunes that are happy and joyous, this negative view ignores the function of the blues (even in its most sophisticated forms). Frederick Douglass once said that black slaves sang not because they were happy, but rather to make themselves happy. Blues, while stylistically reflecting the changes that have occurred in the black social world since emancipation, still performs the same function. It fights oppression not through grand political theory but through the day-to-day overcoming of obstacles.

Murray believes that art is stylized experience. And "an art style is the assimilation in terms of which a given community, folk, or communion of faith embodies its basic attitudes toward experience" (ibid., 84–85). Murray goes on to quote Kenneth Burke as equating stylization with strategy. In other words, the blues provides a way of confronting life rather than withdrawing or escaping. It sizes up the world and thus is a medium of survival.[9] Murray finds it incredible that no Negro leaders have politically used or are even aware of the so-called survival techniques and idiomatic equipment for living that the blues tradition has partly evolved in response to slavery and oppression (ibid., 92).

In fact, whether it was conscious or not, at least one very important black leader has used this confrontation with life in a manner similar to the blues style. Martin Luther King, Jr., in explaining the methodology and philosophy of nonviolent direct action, outlines the necessary steps. They include (1) collection of facts to see if injustices exist; (2) negotiation; (3) self-purification; and (4) direct action (King 1963b, 78). King often stated that the significance of his direct action campaigns rested more in the self-respect gained by the protesters than it did in the actual results of the negotiations. And the use of nonviolence as the means or process made reconciliation with whites possible following the protest. In other words, process or the confrontation with evil was more important than the end. To quote a well-known phrase used by King—"suffering breeds character," and creative suffering is redemptive.

These steps to nonviolent direct action resemble the four steps in the blues formula as presented by Eric Hanson. They are (1) self-analysis which exposes the individual's main weaknesses (self-purification); (2) pain which must be shared with the audience, inviting their sympathy and teaching others experiencing similar pain (collection of injustices); (3) the actual confrontation with pain which emphasizes the process of transcending the pain (direct action); and (4) love or reconciliation as the end which makes life livable (negotiation based on love) (Hanson 1988, 12–21).

Ortiz Wilson supports this view of the blues as a survival mechanism: "They are immortal, not because their lyric content sometimes reflects problems produced by a social-cultural order, out of turn with the universe, but because of the infinite poetic and musical treatment afforded by their unique problem-solving properties" (Wilson 1972, 34). Samuel Charters adds that "the blues song is a sort of exalted or transmuted expression of criticism or complaint, the very creation of singing of which serves as a balm or antidote. The finer the singing of the creative effort, the more effective is the song as a catharsis"[10] (Charters 1975, 124). Thus even though the blues performance is usually a solo, unlike most black music, the other musicians and the instruments, as well as the audience or dancers, are intimately engaged in the action. The private experience of the blues artist becomes public so that the problem may be confronted and overcome through group effort.[11] Jazz represents an extension of this process in that it provides a group form permitting improvisation (freedom) but limiting it to the purposes of the other musicians involved. This freedom of the individual musician may be favorably compared to that of a musician playing with a symphony orchestra in which the conductor has complete control (Jones and Neal 1968, 9).

Jazz, then, is an adaptation of black music to a new environment in the same way that the development of "urban" or "classic" blues represents a modification of "rural" blues for the city. This does not mean that "refined" blues is somehow less authentic or meaningful than "folk" blues as Charters, Courlander, Keil, and Jones have contended. In fact, states Murray, folk music is inherently conservative and necessarily imitative. It was the blues musician who refined and extended folk music in the same way he did the Broadway musicals of white America (ibid., 204–205).

The musicians interviewed by Michael Haralambos saw soul music as a synthesis of gospel music and blues. It represents a union of two life styles that had formally divided black society (Haralambos 1974, 154). Yet the socioeconomic indicators Haralambos uses to link his development of black music to politics indicate no empirical unity. In fact, on almost all measures involving the standard of living we find an increasing disparity between the black middle class and the black underclass. If a decline in the popularity of the blues among young lower-class blacks is solely the result of the demise of Jim Crow, it represents a misreading of the function of the blues. Certainly the themes of the blues remain valid for today's generation. Perhaps the rejection is akin to that suffered by spirituals during the post–Civil War generation. These same spirituals became an important weapon for the army that marched against Jim Crow in the 1960s. Perhaps the rejection is one of style rather than substance. Many of today's most popular blues artists have a larger white following than black. It may be that the style has become so generalized that it has lost its special meaning for lower-class black youth. New forms of musical communication like "rap" records and reggae speak to these views in the stylistic language of the modern generation.[12]

THE "RAP" ATTACK

In the summer of 1979 a successful rhythm and blues group, the Fatback Band, issued a rap record entitled "King Gem III" that launched a wave of similar recordings. As often happens in the record industry, the Fatback Band was not the first or most talented of the rap artists. For years black artists like Gil Scott-Heron, Lou Rawls, and especially the Last Poets have included raps in their music. Not surprisingly, some media gave the white group Blondie credit for establishing this new art form even though their record came three years after the form's introduction.

Most knowledgeable observers trace the origins of rap to Harlem or the South Bronx in 1977. The best known early rap groups or "crews" as they are known included Eddie Cheeba and the Cheeba Crew, DJ Lovebug Star-ski, DJ Hollywood, Grand Master Flash and the Furious Four (now Five), Grand Wizard Theodore, and Zulu Nation (now Soul Sonic Force). These crews and most other New York City rappers used a rapid-fire, high energy (loud) style called "angry." Other styles include "Long Island," "California," or "Country" rap, "Smooth" or "Sophisticated" rap, "Fly Girl" rap and "NY Voice" (baritone) rap. Raps can be spontaneous (freestyle) or stories (narrative) or some combination of the two. Originality is prized, and stealing material from other groups (biting) is looked down on.

Rapping as an art form borrows from several other traditional black folk traditions. Old "dozens" rhymes were public property that anyone could use. For example, one of the more popular ones was: "I'm Hemp the Demp / the lady's pimp / women fight for my delight . . ." (old dozens lyric). Other sources included old playground and "double dutch" (jump rope) rhymes. A popular playground rhyme used by rappers is as follows: "3–6–9, the monkey drank wine / had too much - fell on his behind / the monkey choked so then he smoked dope / and now the poor monkey lost all his hope" (old playground rhyme). When performing a rap, a crew of five rappers (MCs) support each other through a variation of call-and-response known as chanting. Like a preacher working a congregation, some rappers encourage audience participation. Another technique acknowledges people in the crowd during the rap. Early raps were done to the rhythms of special records known as "B-Boy Jams." Many of the most popular B-Boy songs were bootleg records from the West Indies.

Rap music developed out of local block parties in the black ghetto. These parties, often in housing projects, were associated with gangs who occupied their turf. To protect themselves and keep the peace at their parties, all well-known rap crews became affiliated with "security forces." Membership in security force crews like the Casanova Crew, the Nine Crew, and the Zulu Nation ranged from six hundred to thousands. Most rappers were forced to find security from local "stick up kids." Security forces themselves were largely composed of hoodlums, although their energies were channeled into rap competition. Black gang warfare declined dramatically during this period (1978–81).

Like the toasts and blues, rap music contains its share of explicit sex and sexism. Yet, a more positive sign is the advent of the female rapper. Unlike the dozens and toasts which are virtually all-male, female rappers like Lisa Lee of Cosmic Force and Sha-Rock of Funky Four plus One More are a legitimate part of the rap scene. Perhaps the most positive aspect of rap music's evolution has been the advent of protest rap.

By the spring of 1982, Grand Master Flash and the Furious Five's "The Message" became a national hit:

> A child is born with no state of mind
> blind to the ways of mankind
> God smiles on you
> but he's frowning too
> cause only God knows what you go through
> you'll grow up in the ghetto living second rate
> and your eyes will see and you'll start to think hate
> the place you lived and where you play
> looks like one great big alley way
> You'll admire all the number book takers
> the pimps and pushers are the big money makers
> driving big cars spending twenties and tens

and you wanna grow up and be just like them
burglars, gamblers, pick-pockets, scramblers
pimps, the pushers even panhandlers
You say "that's all right I'm no fool"
but then you wind up dropping out of high school
Now you're unemployed, you're life's a void
You're walking around like you're pretty boy Floyd
So you turn stick-up kid but look what you done did
Got send up for an 8 year bid
You're [sic] manhood gets took you're no maytag
You spend the next two years as an undercover fag
being used and abused you're served like hell
Till one day you were found hung dead in your cell
It was plain to see that your life was lost
you was cold as your body swung back and forth
and your eyes they sung that sad, sad, sad song
of how you lived so fast and died so young . . .

(Mele - Mel
Grand Master Flash)

This group has followed "The Message" with other political songs like "Survival," "New York, NY," and "Jesse"—the latter encourages everyone to vote. Run-DMC, the most popular rap group of the mid-eighties, preaches the achievements of Harriet Tubman, Martin Luther King, Malcom X, Jesse Owens, and George Washington Carver in "I'm Proud to Be Black." Its tone is nationalistic, self-reliant, and at the same time receptive to peace initiatives. The chorus is as follows:

You know I'm proud to be black ya'll
And that's a fact ya'll
And if you try to take what's mine
I'll take it back ya'll
It's like that.

(Run-DMC)

In summary, we have been arguing that lower-class black Americans are not a people without a culture. This sub-culture with its associated values and norms has positive as well as negative features. Substantial segments bear the imprint of the African past while others constitute a purely Afro-American construct. It is a dynamic, complex, and at times contradictory culture that does not provide us with a total or fully coherent ideology or worldview. However, it does provide an identifiable style and ethos.

The American context and the slave experience have meant that style or form of expression have assumed political and historical as well as aesthetic meaning. Both white oppression and black tradition have played a role in determining which styles succeed and which pass into oblivion. Those styles or forms that persist may have at their core certain values or goals that have universal appeal. Yet the uniquely Afro-American mode of presentation has usually been the focus of attention.

This form of presentation constitutes the black style in blues and jazz and provides the cutting edge. F. Scott Fitzgerald's "Jazz Age" carried clear associations of a level of culture decidedly outside the mainstream of middle-class white morality (Bluestein 1972, 120). Indeed, it was a cultural level that deviants in the "culture of wealth" sought to emulate—though often for the wrong reasons. More importantly, it was an argument for cultural pluralism.

CHAPTER

3

AFRO-AMERICAN STYLE AND LOWER-CLASS BEHAVIOR

A man becomes a bandit because he does something which is not regarded as criminal by his local conventions, but is so regarded by the State or the local rulers.

(Hobsbawm 1959)

Along with its impressive historical dimensions, the ideology of blackness exhibits considerable coherence, not so much in well-defined doctrine or well-developed system, as in ideals and values, images and rhetoric, joined with the thought of forming a cultural matrix for a new black society. Thus, the ideology of blackness is essentially a cultural phenomenon for which the descriptive word "style" serves as an appropriate analogue for the strategic word "soul."

(Betts 1971)

The liberal emphasis on universal rather than particularistic culture and the individualism expressed throughout American society have served to focus attention on black leadership. On the one hand, genetic explanations of black inferiority were ruled out in favor of environmental or socially conditioned factors. On the other hand, class analysis was regarded as inappropriate in the American context. Combined with the anti-ideological bias of mainstream American politics, leadership rose as the dominant element in the progress of black Americans.

Black leaders were expected to act as models of proper behavior for the black masses. Proper models hastened assimilation, while improper models flaunted independence. In part, black culture aided the emphasis on leadership by glorifying Afro-American cultural heroes. These black heroes filled a vacuum created by the relative absence of powerful black organizations and institutions and the inability of black individuals to participate freely in the broader political and economic system.

Political scientists have studied the development of various styles of black leadership. Furthermore, both black and white scholars have attempted to explain black political activity in terms of leadership styles.[1] As a result, the role of the lower class has been undervalued. Yet as recent research on the civil rights movement has shown, the black folk have had a voice in the political process (McAdam 1982; Morris 1984). Often that voice has been shielded by components of Afro-American culture and interests of the state.

THE ART OF LEADERSHIP

James MacGregor Burns distinguishes between power wielders who may ignore the wants of followers and leaders who represent the values and the motivations of those who follow. One can see in this distinction a contrast between autocratic European monarchs and the traditional African chief (Williams 1976). Yet, Burns goes on to differentiate the transactional leader who directly exchanges valued things with followers (like votes) from the transforming leader, like Gandhi, who raises the consciousness of followers to motivational and moral levels (Burns 1978). Obviously in twentieth-century America—which separates the material and moral levels of existence—the former type of leadership is overwhelmingly dominant.

The incubator for transforming (revolutionary) leadership is a crisis or conflict situation. This conflict may be a personal crisis of the leader or the result of pressure on the society-at-large which makes followers more willing to examine alternatives. Often it is a combination of both factors. Burns cites a remarkable numer of eighteenth- and nineteenth-century intellectual leaders who were marked by internal conflict that expressed itself in emotional breakdown, withdrawal, or alienation (i.e., eccentrics). In a sense, the madman of the theater-of-the-absurd tradition also fits this framework. On the other hand, Martin Luther King seems to have grown into the role of leader as the intensity of the civil rights struggle increased.

The idea or vision that brings about a revolution is not subject to scientific measurement or prediction. According to Burns: "Of all the stages in a transforming revolution the birth of the idea or vision that impels the revolution and its adoption by a decisive number of persons are probably the most crucial steps toward transformation . . ." (Burns 1978, 202). Yet the source of the idea or vision, says Burns, may be as mysterious as the creativity of an artist. Robert Nisbet in *Sociology as an Art Form* goes so far as to argue that it is the artist rather than the intellectual who provides or at least initiates the guiding perceptions of an era. And even the ideas of the greatest social scientists survive more as form than content.

> The Marxian vision is without question one of the three or four most powerful
> and encompassing world-visions to be found in the twentieth century; only
> Christianity and Islam give it serious rivalry. But with all allowance made for
> Marx's erudition and his historic impact upon the social sciences, especially
> sociology, it is an art united with prophecy, virtually religious prophecy, that
> Marxism survives. He was one of those in the century who saw action,
> dynamism, and unfolding movement in structures and processes which others
> regarded as static. (Nisbet 1976, 108)

Nisbet does not find it strange, then, that the young Marx was a Romantic artist
who wrote poems as well as a Romantic revolutionist or nihilist.

Not coincidentally, society tends to repress transforming ideas and those
with the ability to promote them. In his work on the ways in which political
language validates established beliefs and strengthens existing authority structure, Murray Edelman states that, "dominant categories of speech and of
thought define the economically successful and politically powerful as
meritorious, and the unsuccessful and politically deviant as mentally or morally inadequate" (Edelman 1977, 39). Stress is placed on established governmental routines which are highly flexible but also highly confining in the
perceptions they engender. In terms of public policy this might be illustrated
by the labels of "welfare" for the poor, but "subsidies" for the rich.

Edelman believes that the task of the political analyst is to identify the
consequences of subtle symbolism, which is the foundation of political power
and political illusion (Edelman 1977, 155). Unfortunately, much of the popular work on black politics has promoted political illusion rather than revealing it. Most prominent among these Negro leadership studies are the
work of Harold Gosnell, James Q. Wilson, Everett Carll Ladd, and Daniel C.
Thompson.

MILITANT RACE MAN VS. MODERATE NON-RACE MAN

The most striking characteristic of these studies is their emphasis on style.
This style does not represent a particular culture or reflect distinctive group
values, but rather it includes the individual idiosyncrasies of the leader. That is,
the personality and attitude of a race leader in dealing with white decision-
makers becomes the overriding consideration in making the decision. For
example, Everett Carll Ladd states that "a leader may support goals and means
which by themselves would put him in the 'militant' category in a given
community, and yet be regarded as a Moderate because of his rhetoric" (Ladd
1966, 170).

When an interviewer asked a Negro leader why there were two organizations in his city with similar goals—the NAACP and the League for Civic
Improvement—he gave the following answer:

Sir, that is easily explainable. The NAACP stands firm on its principles and demands our rights as American citizens. But it accomplishes little or nothing in this town, and it arouses a good deal of anger in the whites. On the other hand, the League for Civic Improvement is humble and "pussyfooting." It begs for many favors from the whites, and it succeeds quite often. The NAACP cannot be compromised in all the tricks that Negroes have to perform down here. But we pay our dues to it to keep it up as an organization. The League of Civi Improvement does all the dirty work. (Ladd 1966, 232)

These organization styles may be compared to the roles of the "bad nigger" and "the trickster" in folklore.

Another example of whites being more concerned with style than substance comes from Daniel Thompson and involves the "Uncle Tom" leader who is always humble and grateful. According to Thompson, such leaders are often allowed to "get away with murder" because they need prestige among Negroes" "That is, he is permitted, so to speak, to engage in what sometimes appears to be almost radical social action" (Thompson 1963, 62). Of course, such behavior really acts as a kind of social catharsis that prevents the rise of true leadership. In other words, the "Uncle Tom" may be allowed to pretend to be a "bad nigger" for the vicarious enjoyment of the black masses. Gunnar Myrdal views this performance as a game based on "a double standard of understanding and behavior. . . . The white leaders know that they are supposed to be outwitted by the subservient but sly negro leaders," says Myrdal. "They are supposed not only to permit and to enjoy the flattery of the Negro leaders but also to let them get away with something for themselves and for their group" (Myrdal 1964, 773). Even in cases where whites recognize that "their" black leadership is not popularly based, they continue to single out accommodationist actors. For example, M. Elaine Burgess indicates that in Durham, North Carolina, white leaders were "torn between selecting those Negroes who they felt were really most powerful and those whom they believed to be more acceptable to the white leadership" (Burgess 1962, 94). Several picked one individual as "the top leader and 'most influential among the whites because he was of the old school—ambitious but not liberal' " (ibid.).

In a sense, the northern race men or militants described by Harold Gosnell and James Q. Wilson are performing the same function. Gosnell claims that Congressman Oscar DePriest of Illinois was a "race man" above all else. He quotes a white politician as saying: "Oscar DePriest is a race man. I have never definitely found out what they mean by race men, but that is what counts. If you can get that characterization you are sure of getting the Negro support" (Gosnell 1935, 195). Gosnell records that, despite the symbolic rewards, blacks benefited little from DePriest's role as the only black member of Congress. In fact, at the beginning of the Depression, DePriest opposed federal aid to the states for relief purposes.

James Q. Wilson sharply contrasts the styles of Congressman William Dawson and Adam Clayton Powell. While Dawson was an outspoken race advocate in his early years, by the time he joined the ruling Chicago political machine he had become a conservative political organizer who shied away from racial issues. Powell, by contrast, was a flamboyant orator who always took the lead on racial issues.

According to Wilson, both black congressmen might be criticized for a lack of accomplishments. Yet criticism that centers on the nature of their political styles misses the point. He states that "[i]n a situation in which ends are largely unattainable (at least by Negro action alone), *means* become all-important" (Bailey 1967, 161). Wilson believes the political styles of Dawson and Powell are directly attributable to their organizational bases, i.e., party v. church. Moreover, their organizational bases are largely determined by the political system of their respective cities, Chicago and New York. Thus Dawson is an insider while Powell is an outsider.

Although Wilson gently criticizes Gosnell's work for lacking a theoretical orientation, all six works share a common theoretical feature. All six authors believe that style varies with and is determined by the pattern of race relations. And the pattern of race relations in a particular community is determined by whites. Gosnell and Wilson focus on black politicians within the city's white controlled political structure. Myrdal includes both but lacks solid empirical data.

Wilson points out that militants are more often from a lower economic class and different social stratum than moderate leaders, although he chooses to focus on organization rather than class in explaining stylistic differences. Myrdal attributes such stylistic differences to Negro suffrage in the North, which means that not only are lower-class views represented but lower-class Negroes themselves are often elected to office (Myrdal 1964, 733). In the South, says Myrdal, "*leadership conferred upon a Negro by whites raises his class status in the Negro community*" (ibid., 727; emphasis his). Furthermore, Myrdal states that this upper-class Negro is culturally most like the white elite and that such cultural homogeneity is to be preferred: "This can be said positively: *we assume that it is to the advantage of American Negroes as individuals and as a group to become assimilated into American culture, to acquire the traits held in esteem by the dominant white Americans*" (ibid., 929; emphasis his).

This static view of American urban politics conforms to the dominant political science viewpoint that examines the entry of a new group into the American political system as a problem of political assimilation.[2] Obviously, a militant or radical style is indicative of a group not yet ready for integration or even political acculturation (moderate viewpoint). It is clear that if whites control the pattern of race relations, the direction of value assimilation will be unilateral.

TABLE 3

Race Styles in Six Leadership Studies

	Gosnell	Wilson	Thompson	Ladd	Myrdal	Burgess
Environment	Politicians	Politicians	Civic	Civic	Politicians & Civic	Civic
	North (Chicago, 1935)	North (Chicago, N.Y., Detroit, L.A., 1960)	South (New Orleans, 1963)	South (Winston-Salem, Greenville, 1966)	National (1930s)	South (Durham, N.C., 1960)
Theoretical Orientation	Not Stated	Ethnic	Power Elite	Functional	Impressionistic	Power Elite
Focus	Personalities	Political Structure & Organization	Personalities	Issues	Personalities	Issues
Styles	Race Man Non-Race Man	Militant Moderate	Race Man Race Diplomat* Uncle Tom	Militant* (W-S) Moderate* (Greenville) Conservative	Protest Accommodation	Radical, Liberal, Moderate, Conservative
Definition of the Relationship of the Styles	Geographic population	Organizational base	Degree of opposition to discrimination	Threat to the existing race relations structure	Voting base	Degree of opposition to discrimination

*Most effective

The tendency to focus on style in the cases of both leaders and organizations reflects a bias toward functionalism that promotes transactional politics within an incrementalist framework. Wilson's classic work on the political styles of Powell and Dawson tends to promote the tangible patronage won by Dawson while dismissing Powell's rhetoric. Ignored are the relative efforts of the two congressmen to encourage the participation in politics by their constituents as well as the cultural factors involved in determining style. To a very real extent, the church-based militant tradition represented by Powell formed the base of the southern civil rights movement and led to a radical restructuring of southern politics.

It was the success of the civil rights movement that changed southern political systems and organizations and not vice versa. In the North, the civil rights movement and the black power movement had a mobilization effect on black populations. In the first election of black mayors in 1968 and most subsequent elections including the election of Harold Washington in Chicago, the black candidate ran against and not with the Democratic political machine. To argue that the politics of William Dawson would have produced the same result stretches the imagination.

In an environment in which the black politician represents the highest local political authority, he or she is obviously not under the stylistic constraints of the dependent black officeholders of the past. Still, it may be argued that if the mayor hopes to govern effectively or is dependent on white voters, he or she must prevent racial polarization (Levine 1974). The outstanding example of a mayor whose style is widely accredited with his success is Tom Bradley of Los Angeles (Goldstein 1981). Michael Goldstein argues that Bradley's three campaigns for mayor (in 1969, 1973, and 1977), as well as the means by which he governs, have been struggles "to prevent a racial definition of a competitive political arena" (ibid., 142–43). Bradley has refused to take a position on school desegregation plans and the issue of police brutality. In fact, during the 1982 California gubernatorial campaign, pollster Peter Hart contended that candidate Bradley's nonthreatening attitude and demeanor seemed so correct his race worked to his advantage (Perry 1982). Yet while Bradley's low-key style was attractive to over 40 percent of California's white voters, turnout among minority voters was 5 percent below the predicted level (Henry 1983).

The dramatic increase in black elected officials over the last two decades to over 6,000 has tended to obscure the fact that they still represent slightly over 1 percent of all elected officials. Most black elected officials represent predominantly black local constituencies. The election of black mayors, for example, has almost always been dependent upon exceptionally high black turnout in cities with or near majority black populations. Even though most of these cities have historically been heavily democratic, white Democrats have found it difficult to support black mayoral candidates of the same party (Levine 1974; Preston 1982). Of course, there are no black governors and no black senators.

While Tom Bradley has been the most successful big-city mayor in terms of attracting white support, Chicago's Harold Washington and Detroit's Coleman Young have been the least successful. Washington received only 12.3 percent of the white vote in 1983 and Young only 8 percent in 1973. Washington, who felt he was misunderstood by his city's whites, especially the press, distributed copies of Thomas Kochman's book *Black and White Styles in Conflict* to the city hall press corps. Coleman Young also felt that Kochman's book helped explain his problems with whites in Detroit.

Essentially, Kochman argues that the black mode of public debate is animated, interpersonal, and confrontational, while the white mode is relatively dispassionate, impersonal, and nonchallenging. Influenced by the scientific method, whites believe reason and emotion work against each other. Blacks, on the other hand says Kochman, see their emotion and anger as a part of their grievances to be negotiated and not set aside prior to debate. These characteristics almost perfectly mirror media reports on the styles of presidential candidates Michael Dukakis and Jesse Jackson during the 1988 campaign.

This highly aggressive form of public interaction may also include bragging about one's ability rather than possessions, open sexual references from both men and women, generalizations that are not meant to be inclusive, and an emphasis on personal feelings rather than the sensibilities of others. While Kochman's discussion of black and white cultural norms is limited to the black lower class and white middle class, he believes generalization is possible. Certainly, electoral data from big-city elections and the recent presidential campaign of Jesse Jackson indicate remarkable across-the-board class support for black candidates (Marable 1985).

A political consequence of these differing cultural styles emerges in a place outside the voting booth. Law enforcement personnel have taken advantage of black verbal aggressiveness to legitimate repressive acts. Of course, the most notorious case of such action involves the Black Panther party which rose on the very boldness of its style (Cleaver 1968; Marine 1969; Forman 1972). Kochman points out the social injustice of relying on white cultural norms in a legal sense: "For example, both 'fighting words' and 'incitement to riot' statutes make a presumption about the capacity of the 'average addressee' or 'average citizen' to endure or withstand verbal abuse and calls to action" (Kochman 1981, 61). Kochman's assertion that blacks can stand more aggressive rhetoric hides a deeper reality: that is, that blacks, unlike whites, have traditionally not viewed reason and emotion as opposites. Moreover, what has typically been regarded as acceptable aggression or even heroic action for whites has not been viewed as legitimate for blacks.

The "Bad Nigger" Personified
You might be rich as cream and drive your coach
and four-horse team, but you can't keep the world
from moving round, nor Nat Turner from gaining

> ground. And your name it might be Caesar sure,
> and got you cannon can shoot a mile or more, but
> you can't keep the world from moving round, not
> Nat Turner from gaining ground.
>
> (Stuckey 1969, 16)

Eugene Genovese's widely acclaimed *Roll, Jordan, Roll* presents us with a direct contrast to Sterling Stuckey's revolutionary view of slave life. Genovese argues that it was the slaves' adaptation to Christianity that permitted them to survive and maintain a level of morality. Active accommodationism rather than the revolutionary spirit were the motivations to be nurtured.

> The assimilation [of religion] solved the problem of how to achieve spiritual freedom, retain faith in earthly deliverance, instill a spirit of pride and love in each other, and make peace with a political reality within which revolutionary solutions no longer had much prospect . . . For people who even as slaves, were creating an incipient nation within a nation, it would be difficult to imagine a more satisfactory solution. (Genovese 1976, 254–55)

Obviously, Nat Turner's imagination led him to a different solution.

The three best known slave revolts in this country—those led by Gabriel Prosser, Denmark Vesey, and Nat Turner—all drew religious inspiration from the Bible. (They also occurred during times of conflict among the ruling elite, says Genovese.) Specifically the Old Testament stories of the Exodus, Samson and the Philistines, and Joshua's march around Jericho were motivational forces. In addition, Prosser, Vesey, and Turner all considered themselves preachers and were recognized by the slaves as such (Wilmore 1973, 75–76). Significantly, two of the three were also influenced by vodun or voodoo. Vesey took as his chief accomplice the sorcerer Gullah Jack. If not a practitioner of vodun or spiritism, Nat Turner was at least a mystic who merged African and New World religious elements which remain today in those churches closest to the black masses (Tinney 1977, 47).

Vesey and Turner's revolutionary theology directly contradicts the assertion that conjure and religion are fundamentally other-worldly or compensatory. While Genovese recognizes the "religious ideology" of the three slave leaders, he denies that it created a revolutionary folk tradition:

> There is little evidence of a revolutionary folk tradition among the southern slaves of the kind that Palmares inspired among the slaves of the Brazilian Northeast or that Rakoczy and Stenka Razia inspired among the peasants of Hungary and Russia. Songs and stories about Gabriel Prosser and Nat Turner did exist, and some tradition has passed down to the present in localities like Southhampton County, Virginia. . . . But as the slave narratives suggest, southern slaves as a whole knew little about the great slave rebels. No powerful tradition emerged, perhaps simply because the revolts never achieved appropriate size or duration. (Genovese 1976, 597)

While not denying the contributions of the revolts in combating the myth of black docility, Genovese sees as more important the slaves' accommodation to paternalism, which enabled them to assert rights that constituted an implicit rejection of slavery. In developing this notion of an implicit rejection of slavery, Genovese offers the well-known fact that stealing from the master and bending the truth were widely practiced in the slave community. Yet Genovese seems more concerned about the negative impact that stealing had by strengthening the slaveholders' self-esteem and sense of moral superiority. Moreover, such acts were detrimental to the slaves' moral universe: "the slaves' resistance (stealing) inevitably weakened their self-respect and their ability to forge a collective discipline appropriate to the long-term demands of their national liberation." Thus, Genovese's active accommodationism involves little that does not meet with the approval of the master.[3] It is the prototype for Booker T. Washington's philosophy of accommodation.

Ironically, *Roll, Jordan, Roll: The World the Slaves Made* perfectly meets the challenge Genovese hurled at another historian, Vincent Harding, in the late sixties. Writing in response to critics of his defense of William Styron's book *The Confessions of Nat Turner,* Genovese accuses them of insisting "that there was a special kind of subterranean life in the slave quarters which might have proven far more powerful than we now appreciate." He goes on to challenge Harding: "If you say that black folk life can be unearthed and made relevant, then do it . . ." (Duff and Mitchell 1971, 211).

In *Roll, Jordan, Roll* Genovese himself unearths a subterranean slave community that directly contradicts Styron's notion of the Sambo-like slave personality (Stanley Elkins heavily influenced Styron's perception). Yet Genovese's slave world is one of Christian accommodationism that views the impact of Nat Turner as primarily negative. Thus he joins Styron in seeing Turner as a madman divorced from the slave community and leaving no lasting impact. In fact, Genovese attributes much of Turner's current popularity to the impact of Styron's book.

Genovese sees the immediate and harsh black response to *The Confessions of Nat Turner* as evidence of a desire to create black saints. He chooses to respond to the style of the attack rather than its substance:

> It is a book *(The Confessions of Nat Turner: Ten Black Writers Respond)* that demands attention not so much because of the questions it raises about Styron's novel as for what it reveals about the thinking of intellectuals in the Black Power movement. . . . (Duff and Mitchell 1971, 203)

For Genovese, Styron's Turner acknowledges the love that accompanied his hatred by repenting for his killing Margaret Whitehead (a white fictional character). Thus, says Genovese, "he thereby reaffirms his Christianity and his humanity: he sees his own tragedy in his inability to wage uncompromising class war without personalizing the hatred it engenders" (Duff and Mitchell

1971, 211). In the end, then, Styron's Nat Turner fits Genovese's notion of Christian morality.

Several responses to Genovese are particularly relevant here. Mike Thelwell refuses to let Styron's literary license serve as an excuse for turning Turner into a cowardly homosexual. He argues that any book receiving the national attention and critical acclaim that Styron's novel prompts is "no more 'fiction' but a cultural and social document which is both 'illuminating' and potentially definitive of contemporary attitudes" (Duff and Mitchell 1971, 181–82, one might use Haley's *Roots* to support this point). Having attacked the political effect of Styron's historical novel, Thelwell next accuses Styron's Turner of reflecting a white language and a white consciousness reminiscent of today's middle-class Negro. The flat, Old Testament language used by Turner in the novel makes it clear that he cannot preach:

> Anyone who has been privileged to catch the performance of a good black preacher in the rural South understands something of the range and flexibility of this language (language of the spirituals). Lacking complicated syntactical structure and vast vocabulary, it depends on what linguists call para-language; that is, gesture, physical expression, and modulation of cadences and intonation which serve to change the meaning . . . of the same collection of words. It is intensely poetic and expressive, since vivid simile, creative and effective juxtaposition of images, and metaphor must serve in the absence of a large vocabulary to cause the audience to see and feel. It is undoubtedly a language of action rather than a language of reflection, and thus more available to the dramatist than the novelist. (Duff and Mitchell 1971; 182)

Thelwell and others argue, then, that Styron's novel fails as art as well as history.

Vincent Harding (like Sterling Stuckey) is specifically concerned about the historical accuracy of Styron's work. In response to Genovese's charge that slaves and postslavery blacks failed to keep alive "a politically relevant legend of Nat Turner or any other Southern slave leader," Harding cites the inclusion of Turner in the works of Frederick Douglass, Samuel Ringold Ward, Henry Highland Garnet, Harriet Tubman, H. Ford Douglass, George Washington Williams, Marcus Garvey, Sterling Brown, Robert Hayden, Arna Bontemps, Margaret Walker, Malcolm X, and the recorded slave recollections in the Federal Writers' Project.

The debate over the historical and mythic importance of Nat Turner is really a conflict of cultural perspectives with ideological overtones. Genovese believes the real political significance of Styron's Nat Turner, as well as his own "active accommodationism," is its Christian morality. For Genovese it is this morality that humanizes the slave and enables the community to survive systematic oppression. For Styron's critics, like Sterling Stuckey, the significance of leaders like Nat Turner and Denmark Vesey lies in their revolutionary vision. Stuckey argues that Genovese is right in recognizing the universalist offer of forgiveness and ultimate reconciliation to whites contained in black Christianity, but he underestimates the degree of nationalist consciousness contained in slave religion. Vesey's synthesis of radical Christianity and African religious practices, for example, presaged the use of religion in African political rebellions.

In commenting on the absence of the populist distributor type of bandit (Robin Hood) in both African reality and folklore, Ralph A. Austen suggests that in Southern Africa heroic criminality did not present itself as a meaningful response to competition from better-capitalized whites. Given the vast economic gaps between black and white created by the mining industry and the suppression of independent black cultivators by the South African government, there was little hope that direct action would elicit any shift in state support from Europeans. The response of rural black South Africans, says Austen, "was neither the acting out nor contemplation of bandit models but rather the formation of independent churches as a very different expression of resistance" (Crummey 1986, 93).

"Active accommodationism" as defined by Genovese parallels the assimilationist position stated or implied in the Negro leadership studies. Wilson, for example, argues that "politics for the Negro, as for other ethnic groups before him, can be viewed as a set of 'learned responses' which he acquires from the distinctive political system of the city in which he lives" (Wilson 1960, 22). For Wilson and many of his colleagues, black political behavior assumes significance as it conforms to mainstream norms. Black behavior that does not conform to such norms is either not political or dysfunctional.

If crime is inherently a form of protest, since it violates the law, then when laws are clearly directed by one race against the other as in slavery, they promote a race-conscious defiance. The shift from slave to free status that followed emancipation tended to separate norms from the legal order. That is, behavior that was both customary and legal during slavery was not necessarily legal after emancipation. Thus attempts to keep blacks in their place after the passage of the thirteenth, fourteenth, and fifteenth amendments to the Constitution continued, although they did not always have the sanction of the law. After the Civil War, then, the definition of a "bad nigger" did not have to include an illegal component. This same distinction may be applied to Negro leadership studies of the pre-sixties South and the post-sixties South. Yet, the importance of black political behavior lies not in its legality or illegality, but in its cultural content. Do the actions of the "bad nigger" constitute a culturally autonomous leadership style?

BLACK BAD MEN AND WHITE HEROES

Lawrence Levine's *Black Culture and Black Consciousness* demonstrates the changes in Afro-American folk thought after emancipation through the development of tales involving the bad man and hero. Levine states that these tales of black men directly confronting whites largely replace the trickster tales. Unlike Genovese, Levine finds a rich respository of black rebels who were accepted by and remembered in the family and community:

> It was not necessary to transform the traditional slave trickster in order to produce situations in which slaves directly confronted their masters. Black lore is filled with hundreds of stories, anecdotes, and reminiscences which relate with admiration and pride instances of slaves standing up to the whites, inisting upon their rights, utilizing force, dying, if necessary, to protect their family and friends. (Levine 1977, 391)

With the onset of freedom, however, black heroes begin to more closely resemble white heroes in their superhuman feats and exaggerated individualism.

Levine claims that two predominant types of hero emerge: the bad man who transgressed all of the moral and legal bounds of society, and the strong, self-contained hero who violated not the laws or the moral code but rather the stereotyped roles set aside for blacks. The fictional black bad man Stackolee and the folklore based on the exploits of real black outlaws are cited as illustrations of the first type. John Henry, Jack Johnson, and Joe Louis are prominent examples of the second type. Yet it may be argued that these distinctions are forced and artificial.

Folklorist Roger Abrahams makes no distinction between the bad man and the hero:

> He is (the badman) in many ways a contest hero: the hero is placed in the position of publicly defeating all rivals. . . . The rivalry may be in skill, fortitude, virtue, or in main strength but such proof of the hero by contest with other humans is almost universal. (Abrahams 1970, 65)

Thus Abrahams, in contrast to Levine and folklorist Bruce Jackson, does not see the bad man as purely nihilistic, amoral, and escapist. In fact, Abrahams argues that it is the trickster who represents escapism.[4]

Abrahams believes that it is the situation rather than the character of the bad man that determines his action. John Henry, for example, is the hard man but because of his situation he does not need to act immorally, for the most part. His aggression is channeled toward the machine, which is attempting to emasculate him, rather than toward other humans. In fact, in the Philadelphia neighborhood studied by Abrahams, John Henry is remembered more for his sexual feats (Levine's morality?) than for his battle with the machine. And, Stackolee, the ultimate "bad nigger," expects to pay for his sinfulness (sexual and otherwise) with his life. The trick is to die with style. Abrahams, then, sees the bad man as "consciously and sincerely immoral . . . rebelling against white man's laws" (Abrahams 1970, 65–66). Jackson and, implicitly, Levine view the bad man's rebellion as having no focus.

Three real life examples of heroes/bad men further weaken Levine's argument. All three are heroes to a significant portion of black America but were either labelled "bad niggers" or consciously sought such a label. Frederick Douglass, the dominant black figure in nineteenth-century American history, cheerfully accepted the label his enemies gave him as the "bad sheep." Douglass kept a picture of black boxer Peter Jackson in his study to remind himself of the role fists play in solving "the Negro question." He supported John Brown's raid on Harpers Ferry and was disappointed that Brown had abandoned an earlier plan of guerilla warfare. Douglass pointed to his physical resistance to the beating of an overseer as the moment that changed his life.[5] Only at that moment—and not through active accommodationism—is the slave free from the master's definition of him (Butterfield 1974, 25). In a manner carried to its zenith by Jack Johnson, Douglass shocked the sensibilities of whites by promenading down New York City's Broadway in 1849 with an English lady on each arm (Moses 1978, 84).

It is more difficult to label prize fighter Jack Johnson a hero in the same sense as Douglass. Yet Levine chose to do so because Johnson lived inside the law and physically assaulted whites in an appropriate manner. However, Johnson's sexual activities including the flaunting of white female friends, his utter disregard of death and danger, his extravagant life style, and his refusal to knuckle under to white pressure clearly fall into the domain of the "bad nigger." This reality did lead Johnson to break legal and moral codes. More importantly, those laws and codes were established specifically to control him both at the state and national levels (Gilmore 1975; Wiggins 1971). In other words, stereotypical roles for blacks are more than an attitudinal problem. While middle-class blacks often condemned Johnson's actions, a popular folk legend grew up around him:

> Amaze an' Grace how sweet it sounds
> Jack Johnsons knocked Jim Jeffries down.
> Jim Jeffries jumped up an' hit Jack on the chin.
> An' then Jack knocked him down again.
>
> The Yankees hold the play,
> The white man pull the trigger;
> But it makes no difference what the whiteman say,
> The world champion's still a nigger.
>
> (Gilmore 1975, 48)

The practical effect of Johnson's legacy was to popularize sport as an avenue of black advancement in America.

Like Jack Johnson, Marcus Garvey was the subject of various legal maneuverings by the FBI to control his actions. Yet Garvey insisted on speaking out despite efforts to quiet him. Garvey also established a religious wing of his U.N.I.A. that worshipped a black God. Though it was Christian in form, Garvey considered differences between religions such as Christianity and Islam inconsequential. This attitude made Garvey's organization an ideal incubator for budding Islamic movements in the United States. Both Elijah Muhammad and Noble Drew Ali were influenced by Garvey. While Garvey's speaking and writing ability is widely known, his prolific poetry of liberation is less known. Familiar themes in his poetry include the beauty of the black woman, the need for self-reliance, the glories of African history, an end to black participation in white wars, and protests at the Italian invasion of Ethiopia. He was also active during the Harlem Renaissance, supporting some authors and condemning others who fostered stereotypical black roles (notably Claude McKay and Paul Robeson).

Garvey was convicted of mail fraud in 1923 and deported in 1927. The evidence against him was an envelope said to have been addressed by him in which a letter or circular promoting the Black Star steamship line had been enclosed. Significantly, none of the 40,000 stockholders in the company ever charged Garvey with fraud (Martin 1976). Thus Garvey's actions, like Johnson's, forced a redefinition of the law to make those actions illegal. Given the historical record, it would be difficult to label Garvey, Johnson, or Douglass as nihilists, yet they are all "bad niggers."

A final distinction Lawrence Levine makes between bad men is racial. Black legend never portrayed them as good, noble, or innocent. Their morality, brutality, and law breaking were presented without socially redeeming excuses. According to Levine they may be described as avengers or terrorists who prove that even the poor and weak can be terrible. In Fanon's terms, we might say that they erase invisibility by forcing recognition.

In stark contrast to the realism of the "bad nigger" stands the romanticized white bandit. From Robin Hood through Jesse James the white bad man has been veiwed as the enemy of the rich and the friend of the poor. Thus for Levine, the crucial cultural difference in these folk figures is "that whites have tended to sanitize and civilize them, to make them benefactors who dispense social justice to the entire group, while Negroes have refrained almost entirely from this form of ritual" (Levine 1977, 419). However, Levine fails to connect the black bad man's violence to the struggle for recognition (see Douglass 1968 and Fanon 1967). He also fails to explain the need for whites to "sanitize" their heores. Ironically, one of the most universal traits of this type of bandit (Robin Hood–Jesse James) is his adoption of disguises (even women's dress) and other forms of trickery to succeed. This behavior stands in sharp contrast to the flamboyant machismo of the black bad man and more resembles the trickster model. These distinctions remain even today in the accounts of political prisoners (broadly defined).

POLITICAL PRISONERS

On 2 January 1987, the *New York Times* reported the arrest of Larry Davis. A black man with a criminal record, he was accused of wounding six police officers and had—with the help of friends—eluded a massive manhunt for seventeen days. As he was led away from a Bronx housing project in manacles on 7 December, dozens of tenants leaned out of the windows to chant "Lar-ry! Lar-ry!" Davis's status as a folk hero came as no surprise to Claude Brown, author of *Manchild in the Promised Land,* who said, "The white police department has been intimidating the black community—thinking of Eleanor Bumpurs and Michael Steward—and all of a sudden here comes Larry Davis the avenging angel. It's like, 'We finally won one.' " Radio personalities reported an overwhelmingly positive response to Davis from "thoughtful, rational kinds of people." L L Cool J, a best-selling rap musician, reported on the comments heard in his black middle-class neighborhood: "Incredibly enough, a lot of people respect him. . . . He did something brave. Whether it was right or wrong doesn't matter to a lot of people. They looked at Larry Davis and said, 'That guy's *bad.*' Like Tony Dorsett or something. . . ." The threat of violence or prison has no effect in the ghetto subculture to those interviewed by the *Times.* Again they quote Claude Brown:

> Prison, and doing "bits" (time), has strangely ambivalent, perhaps even per-
> vertedly romanticized appeal to poor black teen-agers. It is viewed as an
> inevitability, or at least a probability, accompanied by nothing more than the
> mild apprehension or anxiety that attends, for instance, a bar mitzvah, joining
> the Marines or any other manhood initiation ritual in any normal society. One
> goes to the Marines as a young boy and comes out a "real man." It is the same
> with going into the "joint," as prison is called.[6]

In a massive study of criminal violence and criminal justice, Charles Silber-man attempts to explain, through the use of folklore, the dramatic rise in criminal violence on the part of black offenders. Silberman contends that the great achievement of the toasts (a form of boasting), the blues, and the dozens (a game of put down) has been to relieve black pain and redirect black anger into entertainment and play. However, with the development of electronic media, the bad man (Shaft and Superfly) has been glorified while active participation in black folk culture has declined. Young black men have shifted from the mythic to the real. Like the bad man, according to Silberman, they are more concerned with demonstrating their "badness" (style) than with achieving any goal or accomplishing any purpose (Silberman 1980).

In a sense, Silberman sees the riots of the sixties, Malcolm X, James Forman, and the Black Panthers as "Stackolee and Signifying Monkey toasts writ large." (And, in fact, Black Panther Bobby Seale named his son Stackolee.) One version of the Stackolee toasts ends with the protagonist escaping from a courtroom where he has just been sentenced to twenty years for the murder of Billy Lyons:

> And then—just then, in walked this ho.
> By the courtroom's surprise that ho pulled
> two long forty-fives.
> Stag grabbed his forty-five and shot his
> way to the courtroom do',
> Tipped his hat to all the ladies once mo'
> Down on the corner of Vampire Street there was Stag,
> Old dude called Booty Green.
> That's the cleanest motherfucker I ever seen,
> With a great big, long, white limousine.
> Stag got in the limousine;
> They drove round the block until they came
> to their hideout.
> They was sittin' in there shaffling them
> broads [cards], sippin' that gin . . .
> That's when them goddam rollers start
> tippin' back in.
>
> (Dance 1978, 229)

Thus, though Stag makes a dramatic escape from the courtroom with the help of a prostitute, the toast ends with the police (rollers) surrounding him again.

The Signifying Monkey toast owes more to the folktale tradition of Br'er Rabbit and the trickster than to the direct confrontation found in the "bad nigger" toasts. Still, the Signifying Monkey as a trickster does not always emerge on top. Levine reports on a version in which Monkey is captured and killed by Lion:

> Lion said, "Ain't gonna be no apologizing.
> I'ma put an end to his motherfucking signifying."
> Now when you go through the jungle, there's
> a tombstone so they say,
> "Here the Signifying Monkey lay,
> Who got kicked in the nose fuck-up in the eyes,
> Stomped in the ribs, kicked in the face,
> Drove backwards to his ass-hole, knocked
> his neck out of place."
>
> (Levine 1977, 379)

Silberman rejects the politicalization of the "bad nigger" myth as excusing murder, rape, and robbery as political acts. "From the perspective of lower-class black culture," says Silberman, "the means were the end" (Silberman 1980, 212).

Political scientist Martin Kilson has argued that "lower-strata militant leaders" have stamped "the politics of black ethnicity with a lower-class style" that forces even middle-class Negroes to participate "at least partly in terms of the lower-class criteria that legitimate politics" (Kilson in Wilson 1973, 189). Kilson adds that lower-class black leaders "lack the habits, values, and skills required for a durable politization of the Negro population" (ibid., 189).

Silberman and Kilson reject the "riot ideology" point of view that sees urban violence as protest and as a legitimate mode of making demands on the existing authority structure. The "riot ideology" school of thought rejects the notion that rioters are "riff-raff" or common criminals by pointing to several post-riot surveys which found that many ghetto residents, as well as riot participants, discuss riots in protest terms (Feagin and Hahn 1973, 26). Support for both positions can be found in interviews with riot participants, as was found in Watts in 1965 (the first riot to be described in political terms). At a community meeting early on the day of the riot, a remark was made that blacks would be spreading the violence to white suburbs that evening. Although the remark was shouted down and hardly represented a majority of the statements made, the evening news reported this episode to the exclusion of others. Thus gun dealers in white suburbs were quickly sold out of stock. Likewise, a curfew which had been imposed on the riot area received inadequate media coverage, resulting in confusion among area residents.

RIOT OR REBELLION

The Watts riot participants may be classified according to motives into two general groups: those who rioted because of a specific set of grievances and those who rioted for fun and profit. While it appears that the Watts incident was initially sparked as a result of long-standing community grievances against police, both groups participated. The McCone Commission seized on the camaraderie and enthusiasm of the participants as night after night, for almost a week, they left their homes to assault patrolmen and white passersby and to loot and burn neighborhood stores. The commission tended to view the riot as a " 'spasm' of lawlessness reflecting the violent inclinations of a minor criminal group." Such views were supported by newspaper reports like the following: "At dawn, a soot-smudged Negro youth skipped erratically along an Avalon Boulevard sidewalk. He looked exhausted yet strangely exhilarated. He waved his hands wildly. 'Burn, baby, burn,' he yelled" (Cohen and Murphy 1966, 82). A white fireman said he had never seen such a bunch of happy people. "They're having a real good time with this riot!" (Conot 1976, 172).

Yet the "politics of joy" thesis or the "riff-raff" theory suffer from major defects. To point to the number of youth involved and their criminal records is to ignore the fact that the majority of people in Watts are under twenty-five years of age and that the majority of that age group has criminal records. The apparent joy of the rioters overlooks the very real dangers they faced. By the riot's end at least thirty-four persons were dead, more than one thousand injured, and nearly four thousand arrested, almost all of whom were black (Fogelson 1969, 134). What caused Watts residents to overcome such restraints as fear of arrest and concern for personal safety and to adopt violence as an illegitimate means of problem resolution? What motivated those not present at the initial incident to participate in the undeniably exhilarating "moments of madness?"

Once again the following quotes will illustrate the two sides of riot participation. However, both sides are often mentioned by the same person. Some riot solely for profit and fun, others for purely political reasons. Yet it is instructive to see why throwing rocks at police is "fun." And one must note that looting followed a fairly distinct pattern in which white businesses that had a "reputation" were destroyed first. In many cases the fire spread to buildings that were not the initial target. Some merchants who had good reputations were spared, sometimes because of the action of the rioters, but more often because people in the community protected the stores (Conot 1976, 296). Often those engaged in burning buildings for political reasons could not resist helping themselves to some merchandise before it was consumed. Thus, what follows is a mixed bag of motives and rationales.

Mel: I will be truthful with you. After 2 or 3 days after the thing happened, everybody was getting what they could get; I figure, well, I might as well get all what I could get. . . . What made it so bad, the people who were throwing (Molotov cocktails) bombs, they would give you a limited time to be in there and tell you to get out. (Bullock 1966, 42) [A conflict between those interested in destroying property and those wanting to steal it]

Mike: So we took all the back streets and all the dark streets to the pad, and when I got home, I just sat down and looked at TV, and still I didn't feel, I didn't know, it was a riot. This was the first night (probably Thursday), and I finally . . . figured in the pad that there was a riot outside. At the last minute I suddenly realized that that was where I just came from. So my mother, she tried to encourage me to stay in the pad where I wouldn't get into no trouble, and all that, but you know me. She got to telling me about the looting; there wasn't nobody saying nothing about it. . . . So I got back out in the street again and participated and threw a few rocks, and looted a little case and stuff like that, and . . . I was on the til they called out the National Guard, and that's when I decided to go back to the pad, 'cause the National Guard they weren't jiving. [Gradual perception of a breakdown of law and order until the arrival of the National Guard]

Mel: Heard over the news (on TV) that there was a riot in Watts . . .
sneak out the house. . . . But at first I was really frightened, because
I heard about riots in other countries, but never a riot in America.
Never had I realized what a riot really was. So I went in the store,
and I was panicky. Everybody was knocking down, people grabbing
stuff, grabbing wine, bottles, beer; stuff was all over the floor;
people were just taking what they want. [Perception of danger and
a riot situation]

I had bunches of greens, all in the basket; I had everything, and I got
to my mother's car, put it all in the car, driving home; the police,
they couldn't do nothing. The world was just out of hand.

Chuck: I stayed a while on 103rd, just to look; in other words, just to see if
I could anything I wanted, like everybody, free. (Bullock 1966,
39–44) [Going along with the crowd]

While it may be stretching the truth to say that rioters shared a consistent
set of beliefs that might be termed ideology, it does seem clear that they shared
a common perception of the situation. One element of that perception was the
shared belief that the police were powerless to control the situation. The
police were widely regarded by the residents of Watts as oppressive instruments of social control. To drive them out of Watts or hold them powerless was to achieve freedom. It was to control one's own destiny. Now the
crowd, one's peers, defined the situation, not outsiders. It was part of being an
American—being equal. Bob Bailey of CORE describes his reactions to the riot:

When I saw the police, and they were standing off—way off and wouldn't
come down—I felt free for the first time in my life. I felt like I was really part of
America, and America was part of me. And that if this is what the white people
have been feeling all these years, what a wonderful thing it must be!
    I'd participated in the civil rights movement, but I'd never felt that way
before. And it seemed to me that this was what America was all about. I felt
like I had the Constitution in my brain and that my body and soul were part of
the land—that I owned it and wanted to plant flowers and make it green and
beautiful. And I ran in the park with the kids and shouted Hallelujah! Hallelujah!

Bailey's statement supports the view that portrays ghetto violence as a
continuation of the type of collective bargaining which developed in earlier
nonviolent efforts, as a way of disrupting the affairs of the existing political
system in the hope that negotiation would result (Feagin and Hahn 1973;
Piven and Cloward 1979). However, this style or type of protest was not under
the control of established black leadership and did not abide by the "rules-of-
the-game." Two blocks east of the spot where black leader/comedian Dick

Gregory had been shot trying to quell the disturbance, black Assemblyman (now Congressman) Mervyn Dymally was attempting to do the same:

"Let's cool it!" he said.
"Man! Where you from?" one challenged him.
"You from the west side? From Baldwin Hills?"
"No man," Dymally answered, "I live here."
"You must live in some big house."
"No man. I'm the people."
"If you're the people—" the kid handed him a bottle,
"Throw it!"
"No man. I'm for peace!"
"Hell!" the kid said. "You with the *man!*"

(Conot 1976, 193)

In this case, violence was used as a means test to separate ghetto residents from middle-class black leaders. National civil rights leaders (i.e., King and Gregory), state leaders, and city councilmen had no success in persuading the crowds to disperse. It appears that an onlooker was right when he joyously shouted: "This is a grass roots thing white devil. Negro leaders can't stop this. The U.S. Army can't stop this. It just has to run its course" (Conot 1976, 193).

From the above-mentioned statements and the post-riot surveys it seems clear that significant numbers of participants in the Watts violence wanted to send a political message to both black and white leaders. In fact, increased economic assistance and political sensitivity were a direct result of the urban rebellion (Glasgow 1981). Yet other riot participants saw it as an opportunity for a material transaction (looting) rather than transforming politics. While violence might have become a political statement or style for some, no coherent riot ideology emerged. However, the political content of lower-class or ghetto demands can be seen in the remarkable works of black activists sent to prison. Although one might begin with Nat Turner's "Confessions" and the strong protests of convict work songs, the *Autobiography of Malcolm X* is usually viewed as the beginning of this modern literary renaissance (Stepto 1979; Franklin 1978). Silberman cites Malcolm X as one who deliberately cultivated the "bad nigger" image and was widely admired by blacks as a result of it. This literature in all its forms stresses the injustice of the current social system, attacks capitalism, and calls for alliances among all third world people.[7] The autobiographies of black prisoners like George Jackson, Angela Davis, and Eldridge Cleaver stand diametrically opposed to the narratives of the lives of professional criminals. The latter are offered as lessons learned and warnings about straying from the chosen path (Franklin 1978, 132).

In the field of music, Paul Garon makes the same racial distinction between hillbilly music, which despite some similarities to blues is dominated by guilt and conventional Protestant morality; and the revolutionary character of the blues. Of course, a number of scholars have linked changes in the form and substance of black music to political and social movements (see Porter 1977; Kofsky 1970).

Even the white rebel cannot be accurately perceived from the black perspective. In *Saint Genet: Actor and Martyr,* Jean-Paul Sartre portrays Jean Genet as a man who fights invisibility through crime. As he becomes a specialist in crime, his status increases. As a prisoner he delights in bullying the other prisoners with his knowledge—expressed through his poetry. Yet the impersonal police bureaucracy treats him as an anonymous object. Thus he is invisible again and forced to write books that create horror. Sartre says the greatest tribute one could pay him would be to lock him up for inciting to murder (Sartre 1963). One is reminded of Imamu Baraka's call for "poems that kill." One is also reminded of white convicts like William Wantling who find their only victory in the almost existential transcendence by the individual, anarchic poet over organized society. It is these white bad men who more closely approach Genovese's, Levine's, and Silberman's definition of the "bad nigger."

It would be simplistic and a mistake to argue that the "bad nigger" offers blacks as a group a viable vision of the future. For example, the obvious sexism of the toasts presents a wholly male perspective on entertainment and survival. While the obscene language reflects both ghetto style and rebellion against white cultural norms, the typical portrayal of women as prostitutes or targets for sexual aggression perpetuates the stereotypes of white society. The sexual assertiveness of both men and women in this genre does not compensate for the degraded status accorded women. Moreover, the toasts and games like the dozens are forms participated in only by men. Daryl Cumber Dance reports in *Shuckin' and Jivin'* that she has never seen a reference to a female teller of toasts or heard a toast told by a female (1978, 226).[8]

Today's equivalent of the toasts, the "raps," may have benefited from the increased black feminist activity of the late seventies and early eighties. As mentioned earlier, the music of groups like Run-DMC contains positive references to black women like Harriet Tubman. Black women have also surfaced as performers of rap music.

As E. J. Hobsbawm states, banditry is incapable of effective guerilla organization or effective ideology and generally takes the form of revolutionary traditionalism (Hobsbawm 1959, 26–28). Yet in his individual assertion, the bandit or bad man is fighting for an identity, for the reassertion of lost values. It is this unceasing psychological scrimmage with the whites, which often flares forth into physical violence, that symbolizes the work of Richard Wright (Ellison 1966 edition, 94).

Psychologists William Grier and Prince Cobbs have explored this theme in terms of the "bad nigger" that must be kept inside. "The bad nigger is bad because he has been required to renounce his manhood to save his life," say the psychologists, and "the more one approaches the American ideal of respectability, the more this hostility must be repressed" (Kochman 1981, 55). The "bad nigger," then, is a reminder of what manhood could be and emerges in Thomas Kochman's black style of public debate.

While boxers like Jack Johnson and Muhammed Ali serve to rescue our "manhood," they do not represent transforming political leadership. The potential for the transforming leadership of the "bad nigger" is perhaps best illustrated by the life of Malcolm X. To a great extent it is Malcolm's style rather than his substance that constitutes his legacy to today's young radicals and makes him the single most popular hero of contemporary black poetry. After all, it was only during the last year of his life that he began to move away from the unique religious ideology of Elijah Muhammad to consider possible alternatives. His break with the Nation of Islam is in part the result of the Nation's political and cultural isolation. Although Malcolm moves to correct the political isolation through the creation of the Organization of Afro-American Unity, the cultural isolation from the black masses promises to remain in the form of the Muslim Mosque Inc. It is Malcolm's style, then, his refusal to back down despite the odds, rather than his ideology or organization, that attracts his following. Among those attracted by his style were the young activists of the Student Non-Violent Coordinating Committee who had grown disenchanted with Christian idealism and the style of Martin Luther King, Jr. Can a style without institutional support produce transforming politics?

CHAPTER

4

JEREMIADS AND THE IDEOLOGICAL FUNCTIONS OF BLACK RELIGION

All gods who receive homage are cruel. All gods dispense suffering without reason. Otherwise they would not be worshipped. Through indiscriminate suffering men know fear and fear is the most divine emotion. It is the stones for altars and the beginning of wisdom. Half gods are worshipped in wine and flowers. Real gods require blood. . . .

Her arms went up in a desperate supplication for a minute. It wasn't exactly pleading, it was asking a question. The sky stayed hardlooking and quiet so she went inside the house. God would do less than He had in His heart.

—Zora Neale Hurston
Their Eyes Were Watching God

At the moment (praying in Montgomery) I experienced the presence of the Divine as I had never experienced him before. It seemed as though I could hear the quiet assurance of an inner voice saying: "Stand up for righteousness, stand up for truth; and God will be at your side forever." Almost at once my fears began to go. My uncertainty disappeared. I was ready to face anything.

—Martin Luther King, Jr.
Stride toward Freedom

I was trying to figure out who had made God mad enough to give us all this trouble—one sister wrapped up in a blanket all the time, the other sister unable to talk. I wondered what went wrong back there. There must have been some really terrible people back there. So I thought I would go to church and see if things got any better. I guess I thought that with all these people in the world, God wouldn't have

> time to read my mind. But things did not get
> better. As a matter of fact, they went downhill
> completely!
>
> —Ella Turner Surry
> in Gwaltney, *Drylongso*

The jeremiad, or political sermon, of the seventeenth-century New England Puritans was the first unique American literary form. Traditionally, the European jeremiad bewailed people's sins, saw current social problems as divine punishment for the sins, and saw repentance as the only alternative to even greater punishment. The Puritans viewed their community as a New Israel destined to carry out God's will and establish a kingdom on earth. Therefore, their sins assumed cosmological significance because they threatened the very salvation of the world. Given this special role, it is somewhat ironic that the Puritans saw their calamities as evidence of their selection as a chosen people. Sacvan Bercovitch has argued that the American jeremiad outlived its Puritan origins to become a central rhetorical feature of American middle-class culture. Almost any public speech by President Reagan lends credence to Bercovitch's claim.[1]

Yet the modern civic religion which grew from the Puritan vision obscures the political side of Puritanism. The Puritans welded church and state together as complementary regulators of secular conduct rather than separating them. While the Bible was supreme in matters it directly addressed, the state was left to control those areas not considered religious. In their uniting of the sacred and secular to produce an organic society functioning for a definite purpose, the Puritans were much closer to traditional African religion than to our current civic religion.

Almost every American ethnic group since the Puritans has at least occasionally had elements of covenant theology in its religious views. However, Afro-Americans have been unique in their use of the chosen people metaphor to affirm their inclusion in the larger society rather than their separateness. Their forced exclusion from this larger society, then, has made it necessary to explain why a chosen people has been made to undergo such suffering.

The Afro-American jeremiad evolved out of the Anglo-American jeremiad as an explanation for the collective suffering of black people. In its most common form the rhetoric holds that blacks are a chosen people within a chosen people. That is, the redemptive suffering of blacks is a necessary precondition for American democracy to fulfill its mission to the world. As such the black jeremiad both explains black suffering and provides a culturally acceptable protest against the black condition. During the antebellum period, the black jeremiad was used to denounce the sin of slavery as a desertion of the nation's sacred mission. After the Civil War and with the onset of "Jim Crow" another version of the black jeremiad rose to prominence. This version parted with America as a chosen land and saw African redemption as the special role of Afro-Americans and West Indians, e.g., Garvey. More recently, Martin Luther King, Jr., and Jesse Jackson have linked America's moral mission to its treatment of people of color. The success of these men as leaders is firmly rooted in the black church tradition—in both black and white denominations—which links the moral lessons of the Bible to current political events.[2] Yet this very church tradition, which emphasizes faith, collectivism, suffering, and authoritarianism, poses political problems of its own.

RELIGION AS SUCCESS

When Marcus Garvey declared that he had "been trying to lift men out of themselves," he was making both a nationalist and integrationist statement. On the one hand, Garvey's emphasis on self-help and racial uplift echoed the calls of earlier black nationalists like Martin Delany and Alexander Crummel for "enterprising men who developed their natural energies, skills and 'worldly talent' to serve their own needs first" (Wilmore 1973, 158). Garvey's famous injunction, "Look Up, You Mighty Race," referred to both material progress and spiritual uplift. And when Garveyites looked up, they saw a black God. With early black emigrationist Bishop Turner, Garvey believed that every people worshiped or should worship a God who resembled themselves:

> Whilst our God has no color, yet it is human to see everything through one's own spectacles, and since the white people have seen their God through white spectacles, we have only now started out (late though it be) to see our God through our spectacles. (Moses 1982, 134)

Yet Garvey's black God retained many white characteristics.

Central to Garvey's racial perspective was the American success ideal. And while Garvey, unlike his initial inspiration Booker T. Washington, had given up on blacks achieving their full potential in the United States, he fully accepted success as the basis of equality and recognition. Leaving behind Booker T.'s emphasis on soon outdated skills and crafts, Garvey captured the entrepreneurial spirit of the age. In May 1919, when Garvey announced plans to create the Black Star Line, ships were the preeminent symbols of national power. American trade with Africa had increased from $47 million in 1914 to $325 million in 1920, and blacks were anxious to own shares, stocks, and a piece of the future (Stein 1986, 65).

Garvey's promotion of the metaphysic of success (which predates that of Rev. Ike, Robert Schuller, and Bishop Sheen) had the potential to disintegrate into the materialism of a Father Divine or Daddy Grace. In fact, black leaders as diverse as Booker T. Washington and W. E. B. DuBois thought the developing Negro church to be largely unconcerned with the moral and social needs of the black community. Criticizing the purposeless emotionalism of the Negro church, Washington stated "that what the Negro church needs is a more definite connection with the social and moral life of the Negro people" (Nelson 1971, 42).

Prominent Washington, D.C., clergyman Francis J. Grimke agreed with Booker T.'s assessment: "I have seen enough myself to say nothing of what I have gathered from a large number of competent witnesses, to convince me that the professor (Booker T.) is not very far out of the way, that the number of bad men that have crept into our ministry is disgracefully and alarmingly large" (Woodson 1942, 228).

In his *Philadelphia Negro,* DuBois presented the functions of Negro church-es in order of present emphasis: (1) the raising of the annual budget; (2) the maintenance of membership; (3) social intercourse and amusements; (4) the setting of moral standards; (5) promotion of general intelligence; (6) efforts for social betterment. The institutionalization of the Negro church was char-acterized by the rejection of many attributes of folk religion such as spirituals and spirit possession. Upwardly mobile blacks moved toward a religious prac-tice that consciously modeled itself on established white denominations, while the black masses established the holiness churches.

Garvey tended to view the piety of traditional black religion as an excuse for a lack of "this-worldly" success. His contribution to the materialism of the age was to transform it with a spiritual mission. According to Robert Hill, the editor of Garvey's papers, the incredible response to Garvey's success myth enabled his racial ideal to become transformed into a militant eschatology of racial redemption. He quotes from a Philadelphia magazine:

> Ride on, Marcus Garvey. You haven't begun to spend till you have spent billions of dollars and millions of lives. Ride on, Marcus Garvey. Thinking men and women are with you. Let the Horse ride and hold the balances high that the world may see justice for all mankind. If billions must be spent to hold the balances high, spend God's billions and call for millions more. (Hill 1983, xliii)

The vision of Garvey as the triumphant black prophet of a millennium of racial success had the effect of a religious conversion for many of his followers. Radical millennial sects like the Nation of Islam in the United States and the Rastafarians in Jamaica attest to the strength of the legacy.

Yet, Garvey himself was careful to cast his message in nonsectarian terminol-ogy. Recognizing the threat his movement represented to traditional church leaders, Garvey chose a language representative of a type of civic religion. The formation of the African Orthodox church (AOC) under the leadership of Rev. George Alexander McGuire was direct evidence of the importance Garvey attached to religion. After Garvey himself, Rev. McGuire was the U.N.I.A. official most quoted in the white press and the man most often identified by outsiders who referred to radicalism in the Garvey movement. By 1924, the African Orthodox church had twenty-one congregations with 2,500 communicants, spread throughout the United States, Canada, Trinidad, Cuba, and Haiti. In Harlem and elsewhere, the church remained viable into the 1930s (Vincent 1971, 135–36).

Beyond the church, Garvey's own organizational style indicates a concern for spiritual qualities and "righteousness" not found in most secular organizations. In part this emphasis on spirituality may account for the poor business practices of the U.N.I.A. Garvey is quoted as saying: "We had no monetary consideration or reward before us, but the good we could do our race, for this and succeeding generations. . . . You will say it is bad business. But gentlemen, there is something spiritual besides business" (Cronon, 117).

The U.N.I.A. leadership included a number of agnostic or only vaguely religious people, and Garvey himself had adopted a kind of ecumenicity that recognized some worth in all religions. However, many individual preachers— particularly those belonging to Baptist churches or smaller sects—and the black masses who became Garveyites were deeply religious in the most fundamental way. Therefore, Garvey's theology centered upon the belief which he found in the black folk tradition that "God helps those who help themselves" (Wilmore 1973, 206). The importance of religion to rank-and-file Garveyites is illustrated by the fact that perhaps as many as half joined religious separatist organizations as the Garvey movement declined (Vincent 1971, 221).

Ironically, Garvey's attempt to develop an African Orthodox church drew little from black religious tradition. Perhaps this helps explain the exodus of Garveyites to black cults and sects after Garvey's arrest. Garvey's affinity for Roman Catholicism and McGuire's training in the Episcopal church were reflected in the orthodox, high-church style of the AOC services. McGuire, for example, was installed as the first bishop of the African Orthodox church by a prelate of the Russian Orthodox church.

E. Franklin Frazier, Randall K. Burkett, and others have suggested that Garvey's movement was more religious than political. While Garvey was careful to disassociate the African Orthodox church from the emotionalism and exuberance that whites associated with black storefront denominations, he did not escape (and perhaps did not want to) the vision of himself as a black Moses or a messiah. Wilson Moses calls him an African redemptionist in the missionary tradition of Alexander Crummell, a mulatto-hating Ethiopian millennialist. According to Moses, Garvey's Christian imperialism made it possible for black Americans to participate in their own version of Manifest Destiny (Moses 1982, 132–38).

Crummell and Garvey, however, differ on a key element of the black religious tradition. The former believed that the degraded status of blacks was no sign of God's disfavor. Many black religious thinkers chose to view black suffering as a test or tempering for the noble work that lay ahead. By contrast, Garvey saw black slavery and oppression as punishment for some ancient sin. The distinction is crucial because the former view requires a religious leap of faith while the latter makes no claims on divine redemption. Success in this world, whether it be material, political, or otherwise, is its own reward.

RELIGION AS SUFFERING

Anthropologist Clifford Geertz has defined religion as "a system of symbols which acts to establish powerful, pervasive, and long-lasting moods and motivations in men by formulating conceptions of a general order of existence and clothing these conceptions with such an aura of factuality that the moods and motivations seem uniquely realistic" (Geertz 1973, 90). The religious perspective embodied in such rituals as the sermon differs in its scope from the commonsensical views expressed in folktales. It moves beyond the realities of everyday life to wider ones which correct and complete them. And it differs from the aesthetic perspective in that it deepens concern with fact and actuality rather than effecting a disengagement or complete absorption of reality as in the blues. The religious perspective embraces nonhypothetical truths not found in the scientific perspective (which has no Afro-American folk tradition), which questions everyday realities from a base of institutionalized skepticism. To know these nonhypothetical truths, one must first believe.

The centrality of religion to the black experience in America has been its ability to interpret that experience in a meaningful way. Again quoting Geertz: "[i]n religious belief and practice a group's ethos is rendered intellectually reasonable by being shown to represent a way of life ideally adapted to the actual state of affairs the world describes while the worldview is rendered emotionally convincing by being presented as an image of an actual state of affairs peculiarly well-arranged to accommodate such a way of life" (ibid., 90). In black religion, the preacher, primarily through the sermon, has linked a particular style of life to a specific metaphysic. When black preachers moved too far away from a meaningful interpretation of current events, as they did in the turn-of-the-century black churches criticized by both DuBois and Booker T. Washington, then a Garvey emerges to challenge that interpretation.

The chief function of the black preacher has been and remains to make the Bible relevant to current events. Black preaching is based on the Bible but not tied to pat legalistic or literalistic answers. Black worshippers are seeking the strength and assurance to survive another day rather than solutions to abstract theological problems. According to Henry Mitchell, these needs have resulted in certain strengths and weaknesses:

> The black preaching tradition has been very strong in the area of free, healing expressions and celebration. It has been very weak in making the climax relevant, either to the sermon text or to the reinforcement of Black growth and enablement. It has been much stronger in its capacity to steel and strenthen determination than in its capacity to relate to what that determination should be. (Mitchell 1970, 189)

In short, it has been successful in creating moods which are made meaningful with reference to past conditions but has not created motivations which are made meaningful with reference to the ends toward which they are conceived to conduce (Geertz 1972, 97).

While the classic works of Benjamin Mays, James Weldon Johnson, and Howard Thurman have documented the beauty and power of black preaching, Peter Paris argues that the art of preaching has been developed to the exclusion of systematically developed and recorded strategy of social transformation. Black preachers, he says, have failed to institutionalize a deliberate style of thought and action aimed at societal change (Paris 1985, 94).

Perhaps the most significant contribution of black theology to black folk religion has been the systematic development of the themes found in black sermons. This new theology has attempted to correct the weaknesses inherent in the often spontaneous black preaching style. In short, it has moved black religion from the realm of inherent ideology (folk sermons) to the realm of derived ideology (systematic thought).

Black theology is both a response to the black power movement and a polemic directed toward the white religious establishment and the theological traditions which support a shallow liberalism. As defined by the National Committee of Black Churchmen in 1969, it is a theology of black liberation:

> It seeks to plumb the black condition in the light of God's revelation in Jesus Christ, so that the black community can see that the gospel is commensurate with the achievement of black humanity. . . . The message of liberation is the revelation of God as revealed in the incarnation of Jesus Christ, Freedom IS the gospel. Jesus is the Liberator! . . . (Wilmore and Cone 1979, 101)

Black theology condemns capitalism, does not condemn violence, contends that God is actively working for black liberation, and demands reparations for past injustices.

As a political ideology the above-mentioned positions of black theologians have provoked substantial criticism from white theologians. Among black theologians, however, only one position seems unresolvable: the question of theodicy. That is, if God is black or actively working on the side of the oppressed, why are blacks still suffering? Moreover, why did God choose to inflict slavery on blacks in the first place?

Dating from slavery, for black folk religion the question of God's righteousness and control of history was not one of thought but rather one of faith. That

God will vindicate the poor and the weak is the very point of departure for faith. Thus the "answer" came through encounter, and there was no philosophical resolution to the problem of evil (Cone 1972, 61). However, to suggest that the problem was solved through the act of faith does not mean the question was not asked. Raboteau states that "(i)n the religious consciousness of the slaves, as revealed by the spirituals the most serious spiritual problem was not the battle versus 'ole Satan' but the inner turmoil of a 'trebbled spirit,'" (Raboteau 1978, 258). Cone adds that while the singers of the spirituals saw the solution as increased faithfulness, the singers of the slave "seculars" (blues) evidenced open rebellion against God. Newbell Niles Puckett provides an excellent example of black theology combined with the practical lessons of folk religion:

> the Sea Island Negroes, not fully content with the Biblical justification of the color-code, say that in the beginning God gave man two bundles wrapped up, one big and one small. . . . (Negro had first choice and greedily chose the big one which had a hoe, plough and axe, white man got the little containing ink and pen.) Besides being a slave explanation of the existing social order, this story has also a moral turn in that it shows the evil results of greediness, and, incidently, the reverence of the Negro for writing. (Puckett 1926, 546)

Lay people were not the only blacks questioning God's ways in the world. In response to the prohibiting of teaching slaves to read or write by the South Carolina legislature in 1828, A.M.E. Bishop Daniel Payne wrote:

> sometimes it seemed as though some wild beast had plunged his fangs into my heart, and was squeezing out its life-blood. Then I began to question the existence of God, and to say: "If he does exist, is he just? If so, why does he suffer one race to oppress and enslave another, to rob them by unrighteous enactments of rights, which they hold most dear and sacred?" (Hamilton 1972, 51)

Payne's agony was soothed with the following words: "With God one day is as a thousand years and a thousand years as one day." One of the most eloquent of the black abolitionists was Rev. Nathaniel Paul speaking on the slave trade: "Tell me ye mighty waters, why did ye sustain the ponderous load of misery. Or speak, ye winds, and say why it was that ye executed your office to waft them onward" (Quarles 1969, 120).

While various rationales were offered for black subjugation and persecution during the last century, the problem of divine intention was never solved to the satisfaction of anyone. According to Gayraud Wilmore the problem was transcended:

> it was transcended by a metaphorical comparison of Black Americans with the liberated children of Israel, an identification with the crucial significance of

Africa in the history of the Judeo-Christian religion, and by the belief that God had promised something better for those that trusted him—that the despoiled and despised people of Africa who had been stolen from their Fatherland had also to be delivered from darkness by the light that shone in the face of Jesus Christ. (Wilmore 1973, 168)

Wilmore sees the black theology of the antebellum period as one which justified Afro-American suffering in terms of the larger goal of African liberation. This basic religious interpretation of the nature and destiny of the black race would remain in the twentieth century even though it was articulated in political rather than theological terminology (ibid.).

The beginnings of this transition to a more pragmatic political comparison can be seen in a 1902 sermon preached by the Rev. Francis J. Grimke at the Fifteenth Street Presbyterian Church in Washington, D.C. Grimke pointed out not only the similarities but also the differences between the Negro and the Children of Israel. First, says Grimke, the Children of Israel went to Egypt voluntarily to escape famine whereas Negroes came to America involuntarily. Second, both races were initially few in number but multiplied greatly. Third, the Egyptians tried to systematically reduce the number of Hebrews, while such attempts against blacks were not concentrated. Fourth, while most Egyptians feared that the Children of Israel would leave, thereby depriving them of a workforce, most whites favored having blacks return to Africa. Finally, Egyptians were afraid the Hebrews would join their enemies if war came, while Negroes have always been loyal to the United States (Woodson 1942, 347–53). Grimke's sermon is not only a more sophisticated rendering of the Children of Israel analogy; his sermons in general reflect the use of more white authors and poets in the sermon text. Blacks are suffering from the identity crisis so aptly seen in the work of DuBois and Garvey. Not all blacks are suffering equally. A black clergyman in the Episcopal church put it this way:

> the most difficult task for black Episcopal priests [is] getting their people out of the mental state of "it would have been better if we had stayed in Egypt. . . . Let's face it—black Episcopalians live in Pharaoh's house, and it doesn't matter whether you were born in it or elected to come into it, as I did. (Turner in Burgess 1982, 90)

Varied black suffering complicates any explanation of it in racial terms.

Wilmore firmly rejects the notion that black suffering is a form of punishment. He states that God permits tragedy and hardships to come upon us for mysterious reasons of his own and not necessarily because we are offenders more than others. "Indeed," says Wilmore, "he may even command some people to bear greater burdens than others in order that his will may be made known" (Wilmore in Newbold, 1977, 169).

These "mysterious reasons" are challenged by William A. Jones, who contends that today's black theologians cannot assume the goodness of God because of black suffering. For example, says Jones, Joseph Washington's works do not point to any black liberation in the present or future that would entitle blacks to be called suffering servants. Such a description implies liberation at some specified time, but Washington seems to imply perpetual black suffering. James Cone spends little time on the question of theodicy. He states that the promise of heaven was sufficient reward for blacks to endure their hardships (Cone 1972, 103). However, Jones contends that Cone does not raise the question of *why* blacks are oppressed. Albert Cleage understands black suffering as a punishment for the sin of failing to resist the oppressor. Jones rejects the gap between the sin and the punishment as unacceptable and asks why whites have not been punished for their racism (Lincoln 1974, 138–39).

These arguments tend to confuse the distinctions between suffering and evil. From a religious perspective, suffering is something to be made bearable or meaningful, while evil is to be avoided. The problem of evil tests our ability to make sound moral judgments given the ethical criteria found in our religion. Suffering, on the other hand, challenges these criteria if we perceive a gap between what we think individuals deserve and what they actually get. Jones argues that in fact, prophets emerge only from "gap" situations. There is no need for a prophetic word in the absence of contradiction (Jones in Smith 1976, 6).

Like Jones, J. D. Roberts sees the problem of evil as the fundamental issue for black theology. Roberts's answer is that human freedom has been perverted by self-centeredness and selfish inhumanity. However, human freedom is a gift from God that must be preserved. Blacks, like Jesus, states Roberts, must "transform suffering into a moral and spiritual victory over evil . . . by living redemptively they can use the suffering rather than be used by it" (Roberts in Lincoln 1974, 98–105). In *Black Belief,* Henry Mitchell essentially agrees with Roberts's position: "To be truly made in God's image and capable of choice, man must be free. Therefore, for a season, God is permissive even allowing for slavery and massive White racism" (Mitchell 1975, 20).

REDEMPTIVE SUFFERING AND BLACK POWER

In 1965 at the Garvey memorial shrine in Kingston, Jamaica, Martin Luther King made a speech in which he implied that Garvey had paved the way for the civil rights movement:

> Marcus Garvey was the first man of color in the history of the United States to lead and develop a mass movement. . . . He was the first man on a mass scale and level to give millions of Negroes a sense of dignity and destiny, and make the Negro feel he is somebody. (Burkett 1978, xv)

King's praise of Garvey, the father of modern black nationalism, must have come as a shock to King's followers, who knew he defined God as Integration.[3] Yet King had often stated that no one can give the Negro self-respect, and he continually cited as the most significant aspect of SCLC campaigns the increased self-dignity of the participants.

During his well-known argument with Stokely Carmichael and Floyd McKissick over the use of the term "black power," King agreed with virtually all that its supporters suggested. Yet he opposed the terminology because of its negative connotations in white America. As he related the discussion in *Where Do We Go from Here?,* King proceeded to outline the broad, positive meaning of the concept as it relates to politics, economics, culture, and psychology. In *My Life with Martin Luther King, Jr.,* Coretta Scott King stated that Martin was for nonviolent black power and that he agreed with Malcolm about racial pride, black superior values, and identification with African heritage (Coretta King 1969, 272). Thus, Martin King's praise of Garvey should really come as no surprise.

Beyond their attempts to develop black self-respect, Garvey and King shared another fundamental project. Both attempted to construct a civic religion. Drawing on their skill as communicators, Garvey and King were able to build mass movements precisely because they appealed to the black religious tradition. The historic difference, however, is that Garvey's civic religion has as a goal the unification of the black race, while King's is directed toward a reconciliation of white and black Americans and eventually the human race. Garvey's goal did not preclude the use of violence or at least self-defense, whereas King was unalterably opposed to violence.

Garvey, Malcolm X, and most of the early SNCC and CORE members recognized the vital role of religious inspiration in attaining their goals. As they became increasingly involved in the political world, tactics were more situational than absolute. While the rhetoric was often militant and inflammatory, few preferred bullets to ballots. During the last year of his life Malcolm X made it clear that he hoped that the United States would bring about genuine change through the ballot rather than the bullet. Even while he doubted that white America was psychologically or morally prepared for such a transformation, he included voter registration on the agenda of his Organization of Afro-American Unity (OAAU). Most of his efforts during that period were directed toward having the United States brought before the United Nations for its human rights violations—a largely symbolic gesture (Goldman 1979, 182–91). Black power advocate Charles Hamilton specifically advises against violence on the grounds that (1) many who are theoretically militant would run from a fight; (2) it would lead to infiltration; and (3) violent revolution in this country would fail (Scott and Brockriede 1969, 180). Thus, black power advocates, by and large, join King in rejecting violence, but only at the tactical level.

Black theology proponent James Cone attributed to King the inspiration for the concept of black power and in turn black theology (Cone 1975, 222). Despite their similarities, Cone accepted the use of violence, whereas King was absolutely opposed.[4]

How could King and Cone possess a similar political theology yet disagree on the use of violence? We believe that Cone placed the issue of violence versus nonviolence in its proper category as a strategy, while King elevated it to a philosophy or way of life in his theology, *though not in the practice of direct action.* Cone contended that it is the influence of Gandhi and white theologians which is responsible for the heavy emphasis on nonviolence. Cone made three points concerning this issue: (1) violence is an institutional problem embedded in the American way of life and so deeply seated that it cannot be overlooked; (2) it is an illusory problem involving only the question of justified and unjustified use of force; and (3) it is not the true issue but serves to cover up the critical question of the creation of a new humanity. The issue for Christians, then, is not whether Jesus committed violence or whether violence is theoretically consistent with love and reconciliation, but rather how God is working for black liberation and the liberation of all oppressed people today (Cone 1975, 217–23).

Cone and King share the basic belief that God is actively at work in today's world fighting for the oppressed. Cone believes this fight can include violence, while King does not. Yet neither one can explain with certainty why blacks are oppressed, given God's omnipotence, nor how long they will remain oppressed. In response to these questions which have historically troubled black preachers and led to disbelief among the less faithful, Cone states that "[t]here is no historical evidence that can prove conclusively that the God of Jesus is actually liberating black people" (Cone 1975, 191). King's response is similar: "I do not pretend to understand all of the ways of God or his particular timetable for grappling with evil" (King 1967a, 64). Ultimately, then, both black theologians must rest their political action on the rock of Christian faith. For King, "[r]eligion is like a mighty wind that breaks down doors and makes that possible and even easy which seems difficult and impossible" (King 1958, 30).

While both James Cone and Martin King are political theologians, only Cone consciously distinguishes between ideology and theology. For Cone, ideology is deformed thought that functions only with the subjective interest of an individual or group. He accuses white theology of being guilty of serving as an ideology that justifies white oppression of blacks. True theology, on the other hand, is the telling of the biblical story of God's liberation of the oppressed. Although the poor will not always hear or act on the Word, the social determination necessary for faith in God's liberating presence in Jesus Christ is present in the social existence of poor people in a way it is not present among the rich (ibid., 95). A question that comes to mind is who determines who is rich and who is poor?[5] As one moves from the world of faith to the world of socioeconomic conditions, is it possible to have a theology that is not subjective?

King's answer to the question of subjectivity and the relative nature of justice was to impose a method of proof by which those claiming the truth are tested through the amount of suffering they are willing to accept for their beliefs. Since truth is relative, one cannot do harm to a person holding contrary beliefs. Beyond that King insisted that love and reconciliation are necessary to achieve the Beloved Community. He believed that such a community, although not immediately attainable, is in the realm of human possibility.

As time progressed King's strategy of nonviolence made the attainment of the Beloved Community less and less feasible. The conservative reformer of Montgomery and Albany moved from a position of nonviolent persuasion to coercive nonviolence in Birmingham and Selma. He became less intent on winning the love of the oppressor than on pressuring liberal whites in the North to support and defend liberal black demands. Finally, as the campaign moved north and addressed the issues of economic justice, King became a radical reformer intent on mass civil disobedience or nonviolent sabotage. He stated that all young radicals "whether they read Gandhi or Frantz Fanon. . . . understand the need for action—direct self-transforming and structure-transforming action. This may be their most creative collective insight" (King 1967a, 41). The fine line between violence and nonviolence began to blur as the demands for justice confronted harsh opposition. King recognized that "the civil rights and peace movements are over—at least in their first form, the protest form" (ibid., 48). He even found "a core of nonviolence toward persons" in the urban rioters of 1967 who directed their hostility at property rather than persons (ibid., 57).

King seems to have been moving closer to Cone's position of justified versus unjustified use of force. An analogy might be drawn to the existence of just and unjust laws.[6] However, as nonviolent tactics escalated in their intensity, the possibilities of achieving a Beloved Community—at least in the United States—grew more remote.

Cone solves the problem of means versus ends by contending that God is ultimately working for justice which may or may not require the use of violence. For Cone, injustice is in itself violent. Moreover, justice does not necessarily require love or reconciliation. King's identification of love with God may in the final analysis be more emotionally and theologically satisfying, yet justice is a more practical and obtainable political goal. As King often stated, laws cannot change man's heart but they can regulate his behavior.

By elevating nonviolent resistance from a strategy to a way of life or moral absolute, King removed the conflict entirely from the political world. Racism became a moral rather than a political problem. At the same time King, like Gandhi, recognized that few mortals had the discipline to be entirely nonviolent. In fact it is a testament to King's power as a charismatic moral leader and black preacher that he was able to convince so many blacks to follow a doctrine that ran counter to much of the black tradition from the Old Testament heroes to secular demands for justice. Despite King's power, there is a basic contradiction in promoting nonviolence as a practical political strategy or means while holding fast to an end that is rooted in nonviolence as a moral absolute which few are expected to embrace. Unless King firmly believed that he could convert a substantial number of both blacks and whites to the ideal of nonviolence, the ideal of a Beloved Community is utopian.

THE WHITE RESPONSE

It is in the context of the white refusal to respond nonviolently that King's political theology is most strained. While it is true that black violence in the United States faces overwhelming white strength—as both King and most black power advocates recognize—it is equally true that King, following Gandhi, believed that authentic nonviolence obtains only when one has the option between violence and nonviolence. If blacks do not have a realistic chance of succeeding through a violent course, then they have given up nothing by pursuing nonviolence. In short, they must be in a situation of power in order to be truly nonviolent (Jones in Harris 1983).

Black power, or the lack thereof, illustrates the essential distinction between Gandhi's position and that of King. Indians were the vast majority, and violent revolution was a real possibility. Thus the alternative of nonviolent change had an appeal for the British as well as the Indian.

King apparently recognized the situational utility of violence in his implied support of the American Revolution. By focusing on a more intermediate and political goal like justice rather than integration he might have bridged the gap that separated him from the black power advocates. Much of his northern program encompassed the demands of such advocates. After confronting the great satan of segregation in Cicero, King retreated to the Westside of Chicago and talked of ending the slums and the need for renewed investments in the black community. SCLC's Operation Breadbasket as started by King and run by Jesse Jackson focused almost exclusively on the economics of community control.[7]

Had King lived to confront the white North with a massive nonviolent campaign of civil disobedience—and the prospects were grim given white hostility and the relative weakness of the black church in the North—the result at best would have been further legislation based on power relationships and not the Beloved Community. In fact during the year of King's proposed Poor People's Campaign, 1968, a nationwide survey found that two-thirds of the white population believed that Negro actions in pressing for civil rights had on the whole hurt their cause rather than helped it. This figure was only slightly higher than it had been in 1964. Black people saw the situation in precisely opposite terms, with two out of three believing such actions helped their cause (Campbell 1971, 139).

White opposition to black protest reinforced the view of black power advocates who argued that nonviolence fails to recognize the pervasive effect of racism. For them King's agape fails on the grounds that whites do not recognize blacks as humans; therefore, appeals to conscience are in vain. If we escalate our tactics to the level of massive civil disobedience, we are admitting the failure of rational and moral persuasion and relying instead on a test of power (Jones in Harris 1983, 234).

Perhaps there was no stronger evidence of the moral hypocrisy of many American citizens than the outrage that greeted King when he announced his opposition to the war in Vietnam. Ironically, King's only supporters tended to be the black power advocates the media had pitted against him. By opposing our Vietnam policy, King—who had divorced himself from absolute pacifism— was joining a long line of black leaders like DuBois, Robeson, Bishop Turner, Douglass, and Randolph, who opposed imperialist wars on political as well as moral grounds (Aptheker 1973, chap. 17).

King himself often attacked the spiritual dissolution of western civilization in general and the United States in particular:

> You have treated them [Afro-Americans] as if they were things rather than persons. Because of this a famine has broken out in your land. In the midst of all your material wealth, you are spiritually and morally poverty-striken, unable to speak to the conscience of this world. (King 1958, 17)

Again, in *Trumpet of Conscience* he cites the spiritual poverty of advanced western society:

> Nothing in our glittering technology can raise man to new heights, because material growth has been made an end in itself, and, in the absence of moral purpose, man himself becomes smaller as the works of man become bigger. (King 1967a, 43)

In a sense, we can view the jeremiad as an epic folktale. It contains essential pieces of a people's traditions and wisdom, thereby helping to define them. However, it goes beyond the secular folktale to provide a sacred mission or goal for a society. Myths can be forward looking in that they provide guideposts for acceptable action. The chosen people myth has been a central guidepost for both black and white Americans. Both groups have worn the mantle of "Manifest Destiny." However, as time has gone by, differences have emerged.

With the dawning of the twentieth century, the prepolitical "Ethiopianism" of earlier black religious activists was replaced with the overtly political movements of Garveyism and Pan-Africanism. Yet, as we have seen, at the mass level an essential part of Garvey's appeal was spiritual. The goal of African redemption and liberation remained. But with the coming of African independence in the 1960s a central element of black radicalism was removed. Africans were capable of redeeming themselves. At the Bandung conference in 1958, leftists from all over the world were amazed to find that one of the two fundamental principles of the conference was religion (Memmi 1965, 133). In fact, it was in part the gaining of freedom of countries like Ghana that inspired our own civil rights movement.

The importance of the black church tradition to the civil rights movement is obvious in the thought and actions of leaders like Martin Luther King. It provided the values and social vision that filled a void created by the material- ism of western culture and the narrow vision of incrementalist politics. On the other hand, a successful synthesis of sacred and secular vision must point out the danger of going too far in either direction. King's belief that all Americans shared one conscience that was essentially good led him to project the Beloved Community as an obtainable political goal. The organic vision of the original Puritan community was too narrow to include blacks, and the modern civic religion of Dwight Eisenhower was too fragmented to give more than ritual rhetoric to King's moral imperative. As a result, his later disillusionment with white liberalism in the face of continued black and third world suffering called into question his ideal. Power and justice were increasingly posed as more realistic goals both within and outside the black church.

CHAPTER

5

CULTURAL POLITICS AND THE JACKSON CAMPAIGN

Suffering breeds character. Character breeds faith. And in the end, faith will not disappoint. Faith, hope, and dreams will prevail. We must be bound together by faith, sustained by hope and driven by a dream. Troubles won't last always. Our time has come.

—Jesse L. Jackson
Speech before the 1984 Democratic National Convention

Hold your head high. Stick your chest out. You can make it. I know it gets rough sometimes. Hold on, the morning comes. I know you get tired sometimes. Hold on, the morning comes. Suffering breeds character, character breeds faith, and in the end faith will not disappoint.

—Jesse L. Jackson
Speech before the 1988 Democratic National Convention

A dozen years ago the Reverend Jesse Jackson announced that "[t]he hands that picked cotton in 1964 will pick a president in 1972."[1] Jackson made a similar pronouncement during his historic 1984 campaign and was wrong again. Of course, Jackson and the National Black Political Convention in 1972 did play a role in the nomination of George McGovern, and Jackson's 1984 Rainbow Coalition played a much more significant part in Walter Mondale's nomination for president. The real significance of the Jackson campaign, however, rests not on the presidential nominee but rather on what it tells us about black politics in the 1980s and its relationship with the polity-at-large.

According to Jackson himself, his 1984 campaign was the culmination of a series of reforms aimed at providing full and equal black participation in national electoral politics and begun at the Democratic National Convention in 1964 by Fannie Lou Hamer and the Mississippi Freedom Democratic Party.[2] These reforms have had a number of consequences, some intentional, some unintentional. On the one hand, the number of black elected officials has grown nationwide from a few hundred to over sixty-four hundred. Today, black elected officials have replaced civil rights activists as the best-known black leaders. On the other hand, there are currently no black senators or governors, and there are over three hundred municipalities with black majorities but no black mayors. Moreover, the reforms and limited black progress have helped set off a white backlash beginning with George Wallace in 1964 and culminating with the overwhelming re-election of Ronald Reagan in 1984.

In this context, the Jackson campaign raises two questions we will attempt to address. First, to what extent does his campaign represent the reassertion of the protest leadership symbolized by Martin Luther King in the sixties over that of today's black elected officials? Put in the terms of a Jackson critic, to what extent does the campaign represent a return to the collectivist, symbolic, authoritarian politics of the black clergy? Second, if the Jackson campaign represents a revival or expansion of black political religion, to what extent does its form limit it in attracting white support?

JACKSON'S STYLE AND THE KING LEGACY

Gerald Davis in his book on the traditional black sermon contends that Jackson shifted his style as the 1984 campaign progressed. He moved from an African-American preacher-cum-American politician to an American politician utilizing the expressive characteristics of black sermon performance to achieve his goals. According to Davis, "Jackson's early efforts to accommodate the sermon structure to his political message were 'almost comical'; [h]is metaphors were skewed. His timing was off. His attempts to articulate his hallmark rhyming couplets fell flat" (Davis 1985, 12). But finally Jackson found the right formula, which culminated in his historic keynote address to the National Democratic Convention on July 17.[3] The result, says Davis, was a transcendent moment when Jackson became "a superordinate moral voice for the redress of the gross insensitivities of the Reagan administration and the inadequacies of the federal polity" (Davis, 12). Despite this moment of national glory, Jackson's style was not universally appreciated.

Jackson's aggressive preaching style clearly alienated some white voters who found it demagogic and threatening. They would have been more comfortable with the quiet diplomacy of a Tom Bradley or of an Ed Brooke. Yet Jackson's style was perfectly suited to the media and to the black audiences who greeted him warmly wherever he went.

The success of Jackson's candidacy as opposed to that of other more experienced black politicians rests in part on this very style. He has risen at
precisely that point in American politics when a strong personality commands
media attention that can be translated into votes. With virtually no funding for
paid media advertisements (in 1984), Jackson was able to more than hold his
own in terms of media coverage. Even when that coverage was negative,
Jackson was quick to counterpunch and turn attacks to his advantage.[4] Thus,
those reporters who likened Jackson to the "Kingfish" of Amos and Andy fame
or who derided him as the end man in a minstrel have been struck by his
ability to obtain and use media coverage. Not a few white voters, after hearing
him during televised debates, have commented with surprise on his ability—
perhaps reflecting a subconscious racism.

Though Jackson often tones down his aggressive, rhythmical oratory for
predominantly white audiences, he has never been as militant as he sounds to
many. In 1972, the *New York Times* stated that "Jackson is militant but
nonviolent, good copy but safe copy; radical in style, not in action. The Jesse
Jackson of today is not a threat to established institutions."[5] During the same
period, Harry Reasoner was quoted as saying that Jackson was a good alternative to the Stokely Carmichaels. Said Reasoner, "Jackson makes sure the tem-
perature never gets out of control and he is not a racist. . . ."[6] Of course,
Jackson's preaching style, background, and emphasis on morality bring inevitable comparisons with his mentor, Martin Luther King.

Jackson has often linked himself directly to King's legacy, and an analysis of
the values and style of his speeches over the period of his leadership as
compared to the values and style of King, discussed in the last chapter, is
instructive. For our analysis, we have selected five publicly available speeches
covering a nineteen-year period before diverse audiences. Our analysis of the
style is based on the traditional sermon units described by Davis in *I Got the
Word in Me and I Can Sing It, You Know.* These traditional elements of the
black sermon include: (1) introduction of a text provided with God's help; (2)
identification of the theme along with a Bible quotation; (3) a literal and then
broad interpretation of the quoted Bible passage; (4) the body of the sermon
which moves between sacred and secular theme-related formulas and concrete and abstract examples; and (5) the conclusion, which is open-ended like
most African-American performance forms and often involves the personal
testimony of the preacher.[7]

Jackson's 1969 speech "Know Who Your Enemy Is" was delivered before a
meeting of SCLC's Operation Breadbasket. The speech or sermon (Jackson
held his meetings on Saturday mornings to avoid conflict with regular church
services) contains most of the traditional elements outlined by Davis. There is
constant interplay between the sacred and secular with the traditional focus
on integrating the latter with the former. For example, Jackson's major theme
of recognizing the enemy focuses on white men:

> In the final analysis, he (the white man) becomes the most subverted of all. Because the black man that he abused resents him. The black woman that he misused . . . will exploit him. . . . And he cannot find fulfillment with his wife because he dehumanized her and made her frigid and cold and inhuman. . . . Listen. Ain't nothing left, but to relate to himself, or another man. And try to get the gratification out of money that he should get out of other humans. And that runs you right back to Jesus' position—man cannot live by bread alone. Try it, but you can't live by bread alone.

Although Jackson seems to indicate that the white man is the enemy and black men and women as well as white women are victims, Jackson later gives examples of black enemies and white allies. He states that a black man infiltrated Marcus Garvey's organization and turned over the files to the white man. Dr. King, says Jackson, was stabbed by a black woman and Malcolm X was shot by a black man. There were whites, on the other hand, like James Reeb, Michael Schwerner, and Andrew Goodman who gave their lives for the civil rights movement.

Jackson's conclusion is rather open-ended in that the enemy could be almost anyone or anything (e.g., white ideas). The traditional sermon elements are present, but the sequence is out of order. The real link to a biblical theme— Jesus being opposed by some Jews but supported by a Roman soldier—is not made until the final part of the talk. Moreover, there is no indication in the introduction that the theme has been divinely inspired. Instead, Jackson immediately launches into his "I Am Somebody" litany and declares that leaders can only interpret, while freedom comes from the bottom up. This interplay with the audience emphasizes self-respect, a value found in all his speeches. The other values expressed include self-help, new values (anti-materialism), and interracial cooperation:

> Jimmy Carter, when he was hungry, George Washington Carver's genius fed him. When lost, Andy Young directed him. And when he was wrong, Daddy King forgave him. Little did we know that black people would be responsible for making of a president.

Jackson's speech before a teenage youth conference in Atlanta in 1978 is entitled "It's Up to You." Jackson immediately engages the audience in a call and response. Each of the following lines is repeated several times by both "the country preacher" and the crowd:

> I am
> Somebody
> Down with dope
> Up with hope
> My mind

Is a pearl
I can learn anything
In the world
Nobody
Will save us
From us,
For us,
But us.

The complete litany is then repeated together:

I am somebody
I am somebody
I may be poor
But I am somebody
I may be unskilled
But I am somebody
Respect me
Protect me
Never neglect me
I am somebody
Down with dope
Up with hope
My mind
Is a pearl
I can learn anything
In the world
Nobody
Will save us
From us,
For us,
But us.
Excel!
Excel!
Right on!

This call and response not only grabs the attention of the youth but also reinforces the three most common themes in Jackson's messages: self-respect, hope, and self-help. There is an additional emphasis on education which was Operation PUSH's main thrust in the late 1970s through Project Excel. Jackson warns that we can be diverted from the values of self-help through sacrifice, service, and self-respect by the temptations of mass media and sexual pleasure.[8] Jackson criticized his young audience for spending more time watching television (18,000 hours by age 16) than in school (11,000 hours) or in church (3,000 hours). Moral decadence, says Jackson, has led to premature pregnancies which threaten this generation. According to him, discipline and character are the solution. Voter registration is also stressed as a moral responsibility to those who sacrificed to achieve that right. Once again, sacrifice as the route to greatness is emphasized.

Undoubtedly, Jackson's best-known address to date is "The Candidate's Challenge: The Call of Conscience, the Courage of Conviction," delivered on 17 July 1984 at the Democratic National Convention in San Francisco. Although both the immediate and television audiences were predominantly white, Jackson did not ignore the Bible or his traditional themes. Early in the address Jackson examines the record of the Reagan administration in light of Jesus' dictum that "we must measure greatness by how we treat the least of these." Reagan has failed, according to Jackson, because he has relied on the laws of convenience which lead to short-term pleasure rather than the laws of sacrifice which lead to greatness. Other traditional Jackson themes include hope and self-help. A new theme focuses on forgiveness and is directly related to black-Jewish conflict during the campaign. Once again Jackson connects this theme with his religion: "I am not a perfect servant. I am a public servant, doing my best against the odds. Be patient. God is not finished with me yet." Self-respect again emerges as a dominant theme, and Jackson bases his claim to a victory of the Rainbow Coalition on it. Jackson states that his campaign was a success not because he won but because it maintained its self-respect and moral integrity by insisting on the right to participate.[9] In the conclusion, Jackson says that Jesus was born in a slum, yet his suffering bred character and faith. Jackson also returns to two familiar themes. The first is the dream metaphor used so effectively by Martin Luther King, Jr.: "We must dream of a new value system . . . dream of teachers . . . who will teach for life . . . dream of doctors . . . more concerned with public health than personal wealth. . . ." The second familiar theme is that of sacrifice. As you dream, says Jackson, "you must know unearned suffering is redemptive."

Jackson entered the 1988 Democratic convention in a much stronger position. Having finished second only to the eventual nominee, Michael Dukakis, Jackson represented an entire wing (left) of the Democratic party. Therefore, his speech tended to reflect a search for common ground around which all factions in the party might unite. In fact, Jackson states that "[p]olitics can be a moral arena where people come together to find common ground."

Despite Jackson's success in doubling his support among whites, his address to the 1988 convention contained many traditional black sermon elements. The speech opens with a reference to suffering: "[m]y right and my privilege to stand here before you has been won—in my lifetime—by the blood and the sweat of the innocent" (the closing also refers to suffering—see above). Early in the address, Jackson refers to the biblical passage of the lions lying down with the lambs. This passage serves as a metaphor for the entire speech whose theme is inclusion. Jackson identifies himself with the underclass who must be included in the party. Jackson states: "All these experts on subculture, underclass, I got my life degree in subculture. Looked down on. Rejected. Low expectations. Told you can't make it. I was born in the slum, but the slum was not born in me." The Republicans are identified as the party of exclusion. Leadership is needed to "set a moral tone, define priorities, and forge a mandate for change." Jackson closes with a typical appeal to faith and hope and a typical rhetorical device: "[t]he God we serve, that endowed our nation, did not bring us this far to leave us now. Keep hope alive. Keep hope alive. Keep hope alive."

Clearly, Jackson's style contains the traditional blending of sacred and secular elements of the black sermon. The delivery is emotional and involves the audience.[10] Both Jackson and King tend to emphasize self-respect, self-help, and faith in the future. They each integrate biblical references into their largely political messages. King, however, much more frequently quotes white literary figures and elements of the "American Creed." Both encourage sacrifice and the glory of redemptive suffering, but King is more often abstract, especially in his discussions of love and nonviolence. Although Jackson is called demagogic, he is no more so than King. The black church tradition leaves little room for doubt among those who are called. The new values both preachers push for are ideal, yet they are tempered with a realism that acknowledges suffering and sacrifice. Only one with a strong religious faith can share their political vision with such assuredness.

THE TRADITIONAL AFRO-AMERICAN SERMON

If it is possible to determine when a performed Afro-American sermon is "good," as Davis does, then it might be possible to partially explain the success of such leaders as King and Jackson by comparing their speeches to rank-and-file black sermons. If King produced the model political sermon in his "I Have a Dream" oration, how do other black sermons measure up?[11]

Although Davis's traditional sermon elements vary somewhat from those described by authorities like Henry Mitchell, it is possible to compare themes and the balance of sacred and secular references in a number of published and unpublished sermons.

In *Black Gospel/White Church,* John M. Burgess presents a historical collection of black sermons that give evidence of the black Episcopal clergy's continuing concern for their community. The sermons range from Alexander Crummel's call for a truly democratic nation that renounces slavery to Walter Dennis's sermon advocating the legalization of marijuana. Few, if any, of these sermons take the traditional form outlined by Davis, although they often mix sacred and secular references with an emphasis on the latter. Many of the themes suggested by V. P. Franklin are prevalent in these sermons.

In *Black Preaching: Select Sermons in the Presbyterian Tradition,* Robert T. Newbold states that the sermons vary in method of preparation, content formula, and delivery style. Each sermon begins with a biblical passage and focuses on black political rights and the social responsibility of the church. Most of these twenty-one sermons mix sacred biblical references with contemporary historical events.

An early collection of sermons by black Baptists of the American Baptist Church was published in 1890 by Rev. Edward M. Brawley. In these sermons, educated ministers discourse on the Bible, using few contemporary references. While one might suspect that black ministers in the white denominations would demonstrate more theological training than their counterparts in black denominations, it is impossible to draw such conclusions from the published sources. However, these sources do reveal more of a concern with identity on the part of black ministers in the white denominations, perhaps reflecting greater insecurity on their part.

Alfred T. Davies has collected a group of interdenominational sermons by both blacks and whites that focus specifically on race. These sermons by well-known religious leaders like Martin Luther King, Jr., and Gardner Taylor tend to view racism and segregation as a religious (moral) problem. Taylor, for example, states that "the problem of people accepting one another is religious" (Davies 1965, 188).

In *Outstanding Black Sermons,* J. Alfred Smith, Sr., presents the sermons of less-known black, mostly Baptist ministers. Only two of these thirteen sermons center on personal development. The other eleven sermons mix sacred and secular references as they develop the activist themes of black pride, church responsibility, and social vision. Rev. Effie Clark, for example, states that "[a]n oppressed people cannot understand the nature of their oppression before they are inspired with hope and a vision of the freedom that they desire. To understand the nature of their oppression, a people must first know who they are; they must also know who their enemy is" (Smith 1976, 25). Rev. Smith helps to identify the enemy in his sermon: "[i]f the black church is to have a worthwhile future, it must redefine theological concepts, like sin, into concrete expressive language. The children of the devil become the narcotic pushers or the pimps" (ibid., 75).

The collected sermons of such early church leaders as Daniel Payne (A.M.E.) and Francis Grimke (Presbyterian) are similar in their emphasis on the moral uplift of Afro-Americans. Yet these two leaders do not ignore governmental responsibility or white racism in addressing black status. More contemporary sermons tend to emphasize the role of the system in black oppression but do not neglect black responsibility.

Manuel Scott's sermons delivered at the Calvary Baptist Church in Los Angeles in the 1960s adhere more closely to the traditional performance form outlined by Davis than any of the other sermons we have reviewed. Starting with a biblical verse, Scott weaves a sermon composed of both sacred and secular references that illustrate his theme. The themes include nonviolence, identity, and brotherhood, with references from Karl Barth, Søren Kierkegaard and Paul Tillich.

One of the most widely heard and hence influential black ministers was William Holmes Borders, whose sermons at the Wheat Street Baptist Church in Atlanta in the 1930s and 1940s were broadcast over the radio. Borders is as comfortable with historical references to the Greeks, the Romans, Hitler, and Roosevelt, and to secular authors like Victor Hugo and Matthew Arnold, as he is with sacred text. His themes range from the low wages and lack of recreational facilities for blacks in Atlanta to the supposed superiority of Germany and the five evils of Western Civilization. In Borders's sermons we find language later used by King ("let freedom ring") and Jackson ("I am somebody").

Two sets of unpublished sermons also help illustrate the transition from moral uplift to more external political activism.[12] John Albert Johnson was born in Ontario, Canada, in 1857 and joined the British Methodist Episcopal Church in 1874. After preaching in Toronto, he was sent to the bishopric of Norfolk, Virginia, in 1908 and later was elected bishop for South Africa. More than one hundred Johnson sermons are held in the Schomburg Collection of the New York Public Library, and they are largely sacred in theme. While Johnson explicitly states that the ministry must concern itself with the secular, he says that the individual has duties as well as rights. Johnson's sermons recognize the complexity of man's nature and the scientific world but tend to concentrate on the development of moral character. In fact, says Johnson, personal progress and national progress are dependent on moral character.

By contrast, the sermons of Egbert Ethelred Brown were almost equally secular or mixed in theme rather than purely sacred. Brown was born in Falmouth, Jamaica, in 1875 and changed his church affiliation from A.M.E. to Unitarian when he was dismissed from the civil service. Ordained in the United States in 1912, he returned to Jamaica to preach until 1920, when once again he returned to the United States, where he founded the Harlem Community Church. The church changed its name to the Hubert Harrison Memorial Church in 1928 and had as founding members such black leftists as W. A. Domingo, Frank Crosswaith, Grace P. Campbell, and Richard B. Moore. Not surprisingly, one of Brown's sermons attacks the leadership of Marcus Garvey. Brown also served as the chief fundraiser in the United States for Norman Manley's People's National party in Jamaica.

Brown revealed a fondness for Ralph Waldo Emerson and was as likely to begin a sermon with a poem as a biblical verse. He viewed the church as a forum for critical thinking and promoted a diversity of religious views. Drawing an analogy between the many denominations and the instruments that comprise an orchestra, Brown stated that we all have a part to play. In a sermon delivered at the Abyssinian Baptist Church, he stressed the need for religious ethics in business and politics and ended by quoting St. Paul on reaping what you sow. This collection of nearly one hundred sermons shows a well-rounded minister who sought to challenge his congregation with references from Tennyson to Michael Servetus (Unitarian martyr) and from the threat of the Catholic church to the threat of Communism.

The sermons reviewed here do not focus exclusively on the themes presented by V. P. Franklin in *Black Self-Determination*. While those values Franklin lists—survival with dignity, resistance against oppression, religious self-determination, and freedom—were often present, other common themes included black identity and moral uplift. Certain themes may appear more frequently during certain historical periods, but those cited by Franklin, along with identity and uplift, are present in every historical period.

A significant number of the sermons we reviewed did not begin with the traditional biblical verse. Of the nearly one hundred sermons that did draw their theme from sacred text, the New Testment was slightly favored over the Old Testament.[13] Matthew was cited in eleven sermons followed by Luke and John with ten citations each. No other New Testament book had more than five citations. Genesis was the favorite Old Testament book, with eight citations, followed by Ezekiel with five and Psalms with four.

While it is impossible to say that these sermons are representative of the black church tradition, the very fact of their availability suggests that they have been influential. They reveal a remarkable diversity of sacred and secular references that are most often combined to deliver a figurative message. In *The Social Teaching of Black Churches,* Peter Paris contends that an ideal hope tempered with realism was the only viable alternative for blacks. This hope was rooted in the religious belief that perfect justice is promised in the kingdom of God and politically grounded in the promises of equality in the American Constitution. Despite their different origins, blacks tended to combine them, says Paris: "[t]he difference between the religious and political views lay in the fact that the first was grounded in an unshakable eschatological faith that admitted no uncertainty, while the latter was rooted in a political document that served the race as an unfulfilled promise. For the most part, however, blacks tended to unite their eschatological and political visions, whereby political realism was subsumed into political idealism" (Paris 1985, 84). As such, they represent a tradition easily adapted to political use.

STYLE AND CHARISMA

Political scientist Adolph Reed, Jr., likens Jackson to Wallace, Carter, and Reagan in his identification with certain collectively held values rather than an instrumental agenda. In a very real sense this is true because such values are more widely shared than specific policies or programs. Ironically, Reagan, a divorced Hollywood actor, presided over an uneasy coalition of East Coast businessmen and fundamentalist southern religious activists, while Jackson, a southern, country preacher, attempted to unite gays, feminists, and Arab-Americans with traditional Democratic groups.

By using his personality and preaching style, Jackson was able to take progressive stands on issues, and at the same time focus on traditional black family values without taking the anti-abortion, anti-gay rights, and pro-death penalty positions often associated with the black church and the black community. In a similar vein, by pushing a progressive foreign policy and attacking Reagan's civil rights record, Jackson was able to avoid issues like busing, which have divided the black community in the past.[14] On social issues, the *National Journal* reports that the Hart delegates to the 1984 convention were more liberal than either Jackson's or Mondale's delegates.[15] Historically, Jackson has refused to push issues like integrated housing in Chicago—the very issue that brought Martin Luther King to that city in 1966. Jackson has preferred to work on black business development while maintaining good relations with groups ranging from black youth gangs and the Nation of Islam to the Chicago Urban League and black ministers.

Jackson's skill in unifying these diverse ideological tendencies is best seen in his support among leading black nationalists like Maulana Karenga (founder of US and creator of Kwanzaa) and Louis Farrakhan (leader of the Nation of Islam). The symbolic importance of a union between a disciple of King and the disciple of the Honorable Elijah Muhammad made it that much more difficult for Jackson to sever his relations with Farrakhan. The fact that Jackson ultimately did sever these relationships was due more to the strategic needs and experience of each leader than it was to ideological incompatibility.[16] The symbolic importance of this unity cannot be downplayed.

One of Jackson's major critics, Adolph Reed, Jr., has argued that the 1984 campaign was a "ritualistic event—a media conveyed politics of symbolism, essentially tangential to the critical debate over reorganization of American capitalism's governing consensus."[17] Reed adds that Jackson's leadership style is anti-democratic and organic in nature.[18] Reed's criticisms make two assumptions: that symbolic politics are not a part of the debate over the direction of American politics, and that collectively held values have no place in agenda building. If one accepts these assumptions as incrementalists often do, then Reed is correct in criticizing Jackson's effort. However, if one acknowledges the linkages between the symbolic and the substantive as well as between the sacred and the secular, as we have done throughout this study and as the tradition of the Afro-American jeremiad does, then the Jackson campaign represents a logical extension of black cultural politics with system transforming potential.

V. P. Franklin has contended that Afro-Americans through slavery and freedom have consistently valued survival with dignity (self-respect), resistance against oppression (self-help), religious self-determination (moral autonomy), and freedom (justice). Franklin states that Booker T. Washington appealed to black self-determination but did not represent blacks' values and interests and therefore was not their leader. Frederick Douglass and W. E. B. DuBois, by contrast, shared all of their values except self-determination, thus weakening their mass appeal. Garvey, says Franklin, was most successful because his ideology and programs strongly appealed to both the interests and the cultural values of late nineteenth-century blacks. Garvey's fatal weakness was an un-familiarity with Afro-American history that led him to embrace the Ku Klux Klan—an action that was programmatically rational but ideologically suicidal. According to Franklin, Martin Luther King was successful with an integrationist movement because black attitudes toward separation had changed with feder-al support for black rights during the New Deal.[19]

If Jackson is to be placed among the ranks of such leaders, his values fall clearly into the tradition described by Franklin. This tradition does not represent an authoritarian, symbolic church style as such, since Douglass, DuBois, and Garvey were not ordained ministers. Rather it reflects a remark-ably consistent blending of sacred and secular values into a pragmatic politics. It is not so much anti-democratic as it is charismatic. And it is ritualistic, but in the sense that it affirms black dignity and selfhood that have been denied by racism.

The charismatic aspects of black leadership are well known and given special emphasis because of the strong link between the black church and politics. However, Aaron Wildavsky in *The Nursing Father: Moses as a Politi-cal Leader* ties leadership style to the way in which regimes are constituted. Regimes in turn are subsumed under a political culture of which there are three basic types according to Wildavsky:

> A hierarchical political culture favors equality before the law so as to adjudi-cate statuses—who has the right to do what—in order to maintain social differences. A culture of competitive individualism supports equality of oppor-tunity, conceived as the ability to enter markets, so that winners can gain more than losers. A sectarian culture values equality of results so as to reduce differences among people. (1984, 23)

Wildavsky presents us with three differing definitions of the concept of equal-ity that depend on the political culture. Martin Luther King's definition—which opened this work—reflects the political culture labeled sectarian by Wildavsky. According to him, only this culture has a need to produce charismatic political leaders. Yet obviously King's cultural values are not dominant, but America has produced white political leaders it calls charismat-ic.

Ann Ruth Willner in *The Spellbinders* discusses Franklin D. Roosevelt as a charismatic leader. Moreover, political leaders from nonsectarian cultures, such as Khomeini, Hitler, and Mussolini, are categorized as charismatic. Will-ner's work moves in an opposite direction from Wildavsky's as she attempts to separate charismatic leadership from environmental factors and place it within the character of the leader. Yet the leader's success is dependent on his or her understanding and exploitation of the culture. Specifically, Willner describes four core factors in charismatic leadership: (1) the assimilation of a leader to one or more of the dominant myths of his or her society and culture; (2) the performance of what appears to be an extraordinary or heroic feat; (3) the projection of the possession of qualities with an uncanny or a powerful aura; and (4) the possession of outstanding rhetorical ability (Willner 1984, 61). While it would be possible to discuss a number of black leaders in relation to these factors, we are here concerned only with the rhetorical power of the black sermon.

According to Willner, "rhetorical spellbinding and the charismatic affect it can induce are produced less by logic and ideas than by emotional stimuli, by words as symbols of more than their literal meaning, in short, by the style of verbal communication" (Willner, 152). Aspects of this style that produce the charismatic affect include the issue of figurative language (usually culturally-loaded), the level of language (i.e., literary or colloquial), and rhetorical devices such as rhythm, repetition, alliteration, and balance. Although each of these elements may have particular implications in the oral traditions of particular cultures, says Willner, there are fewer barriers to cross-cultural understanding of sound devices.[20]

STYLE AND SUBSTANCE IN THE POLITICAL CAMPAIGN

When Jesse Jackson announced his candidacy for president in 1984, the Reverend Benjamin F. Chavis, deputy director of the Commission for Racial Justice of the United Church of Christ, immediately identified his speech as "liberation theology." "His address," says Chavis, "was more of a sermon, in the tradition of great black Baptist preachers, than a speech by an aspiring politician"[21] (Marable 1985, 271). The audience shouted "Amen" and the entire black church community mobilized. Within two months of his announcement, over 90 percent of the black clergy in the U.S. had endorsed him. His campaign manager, Arnold Pickney, compared the significance of the church endorsements to an AFL-CIO endorsement for any other candidate (Marable 1985, 272).

The enthusiasm expressed for Jackson's candidacy by the black church was quickly extended to the black electorate at-large. Black turnout jumped from 8.3 million in 1980 to 10.3 million. In terms of the voting-age population, black participation increased from 50.5 to 55.8 percent, a gain of 5.3 percentage points (white registration gained only 0.5 percentage points) (Cavanagh 1985, 12). Black registration in the South grew by some 695,000 persons over the four years. White registration declined by 227,000 over the same period (Cavanagh and Foster 1984, 16).

Nationally, CBS found that from 4 to 11 percent of black voters were voting for the first time, while in some states like Florida and Georgia, 20 percent of the voters were newly registered. Overall, black primary turnout was dramatically higher than in 1980 (18 percent of the total Democratic primary vote), and the black share of the national vote exceeded one-tenth of the total electorate for the first time.

Most studies give Jackson's candidacy a large share of the credit for stimulating this unprecedented black electoral activity. Sixty-seven percent of newly registered blacks in a survey by the Committee for the Study of the American Electorate cited the Jackson campaign as an important influence on their decision to register. Moreover, the Jackson campaign succeeded in registering a considerable number of blacks whose attachments to the political system had previously been marginal (Cavanagh 1985, 15). This finding supports Willner's assertion that charisma stimulates political activism on the part of many people who had been apolitical or politically apathetic (Willner 1984, 195).

Over the last 20 years the turnout rate for black women has gone from 1.1 percentage points less than that of black men to 7.5 percentage points higher than that of black men. This gap is not fully explained by class status or feminist beliefs (Cavanagh 1985, 16–17). However, it is consistent with the disproportionate share of black church activity carried on by black women.[22] Jackson also received disproportionate support from younger blacks, from blacks whose family financial situation had failed to improve during Reagan's presidency, and from southern blacks (Cavanagh 1985, 30). Such data refute arguments that young blacks cannot identify with a black church style of leadership. They also indicate that Jackson may have enjoyed his greatest strength in the traditional "black Bible belt" of the South.

Although many black leaders had questions about Jackson's personal attributes, the rank-and-file of black voters preferred him greatly over Mondale. His 84 percent or more positive rating on each of 13 positive attributes by blacks surveyed are figures researchers say "one might associate with the Second Coming" (Cavanagh 1985, 30).

Most white voters did not view Jackson's campaign as the Second Coming. While Jackson received 85 percent of the black vote nationwide, his support was much more limited. About 22 percent or 737,000 voters out of a total of 3.4 million Jackson voters were white. (Table 4 provides a state-by-state breakdown along racial lines of voting percentages for Jackson.)

Jackson's limited appeal to white voters should come as no surprise to those familiar with the election campaigns of black big-city mayors. Running in heavily Democratic cities, Democratic black mayoral candidates have received only 9 to 23 percent of the white vote.[23] The one exception has been Tom Bradley of Los Angeles, who lost his first bid for mayor to the incumbent Sam Yorty but has attracted a plurality of white support in subsequent elections.

Racism hampered Jackson's chances as well as those of white candidates identified with him. Among whites, 17 percent said they were less likely to vote for Mondale because of Jackson's endorsement, while only 10 percent were attracted to Mondale as a result of Jackson's support (JCPS 1984, 9). A Joint Center for Political Studies/Gallup survey on perceptions of Jackson,

TABLE 4

1984 Democratic Presidential Primary Votes for Jackson by Race

State	Blacks	Whites
Alabama	50%	1%
California	78	9
Georgia	61	1
Illinois	79	4
Indiana	71	3
Maryland	83	5
New Jersey	86	4
New York	87	6
North Carolina	84	3
Ohio	81	5
Pennsylvania	77	4
Tennessee	76	2
Texas*	83	4

*Sample of caucus participants
Source: CBS/New York *Times* exit survey

Mondale, and Reagan by race found Jackson scoring highest among whites on the attribute of "hard-working" (78%) and lowest on "clear on issues" (33%) and "cares about people like me" (37%). These low figures may represent an inability among white voters to understand Jackson's presentation of issues and to identify with his style.

White ambiguity about Jackson's position on issues is revealing. First, there was little in Jackson's domestic policy pronouncements to distinguish him from candidates like George McGovern. While calling for a halt to Reagan's cutbacks in social welfare programs, the black candidate did not advance specific major new spending programs like full employment or national health insurance.

The real policy distinctions between Jackson and the other presidential candidates were in the area of foreign affairs. In his trips to Syria and Cuba, his opposition to the invasion of Grenada, his support for a Palestinian homeland, and his call for an absolute reduction in military spending, Jackson staked out a clear, leftist position. On the issues of South Africa and a nuclear weapons freeze, Jackson did get some response, but in general his foreign policy positions did little more than attract media attention. Historically, elections are not won on foreign policy concerns, which remain low priority items to most voters.[24] Even the left—which gives high priority to such issues—responded slowly to Jackson's initiatives.[25] Jackson's style, like King's, is rooted in the black church, which often makes the political left uncomfortable.

Second, whites and blacks assigned radically different priorities to campaign issues. The JCPS/Gallup survey asked both groups to name the three most important issues of the presidential campaign. Blacks gave unemployment top priority (65%) followed by government programs to help the poor (45%) and civil rights (38%). Whites divided almost evenly among unemployment (42%), the federal deficit (42%), and inflation (40%). While only 6 percent of whites named civil rights as one of the three major issues, Jackson seemed to tie the success of his campaign to it. Specifically, he linked the collective self-respect and moral integrity of his campaign to the issue of fairness or justice within the Democratic party and the convention itself. This issue had resonance for Afro-American politics but was not deeply felt by non-blacks. Thus, any black candidate—regardless of style—who based his or her campaign on issues relevant to the black community would find significantly less support among whites.

In a similar fashion, a substantial segment of the white population would not vote for any black presidential candidate. Marable quotes an April 1984 poll in which 18 percent of all whites said "they would not vote for a Black man for President, even if he were qualified and was a party nominee" (1985, 282). The JCPS/Gallup survey in 1984 found 18 percent of white respondents were unwilling to vote for a black presidential candidate, and 7 percent "don't know" (and were presumed to be opposed to such candidates). Cavanagh notes that a similar survey in 1958 found over half of the electorate (53%) opposed to a qualified black candidate.

When President Eisenhower uttered his well-known statement, "America was founded on a belief in God—and I don't care what it is," he was expressing a profoundly different type of political or civic religion than King or Jackson. Traditional mainstream white denominations have served a dual function. They have supplied our national quest for identity with a sense of moral uniqueness or superiority (i.e., jeremiad), while at the same time helping many ethnic groups preserve a sense of cultural identity without threatening national unity. Hence, the necessary separation of church and state at the formal level coexists with the delicate call to a national mission or destiny at the ceremonial level.

In the United States, religion has played a primary cultural role in determining or expressing social rationality. The creation of a civic religion meant that the image of God in American political speeches and documents had to be regularized to fit into the existing rational-legal structures (Morris 1974, 48). In short, in the mix of sacred and secular elements, the secular elements contained the real political content, while the sacred elements became public ritual. As practiced, this civic religion was cool, detached, and gave moral support to existing law.

The black challenge to the status quo which peaked in the 1960s questioned both the form of this civic religion and its willingness to live up to its stated objectives. The form of black protest implied a different mix of sacred and secular elements. God was alive and working for the oppressed. The legal-rational order was not seen as morally sanctioned unless the promise of the Constitution was fulfilled. According to John F. Wilson, in *Public Religion in American Culture*, the results were culturally decisive:

> If civil struggle of the nineteenth century secured the unity of the nations as a religious entity—albeit with Church and State separated—the civil struggle of the twentieth century finally rendered that religious basis for unity broken and ineffective. (1979, 17)

Robert Bellah, for one, has seen the resurgence of religious fundamentalism in the 1970s and 1980s as an attempt to recapture the Protestant hegemony of the pre-sixties era.

In large part, the 1984 Jackson campaign was an attempt to recapture the moral hegemony that was briefly enjoyed during the civil rights movement. We have seen that Jackson's political sermons shared few structural elements with the traditional Afro-American sermon. Only in their reliance on biblical verse and in their mix of sacred and secular elements are they traditional. In terms of style there are many more shared characteristics. Jackson's use of rhythm and rhyme, his interplay with the audience, and his use of music and prayer are all very traditional. Moreover, Jackson's themes of self-respect, self-help, hope, and redemptive suffering have deep roots in the black religious tradition.

Jackson's 1984 campaign symbolized a black version of America's civic religion. And while Jackson was able to raise awareness on issues like South Africa and run-off elections, which would have been ignored during the campaign, he was not able to attract significant numbers of whites with his moral vision. While King was often more abstract and integrative in his use of references than Jackson, it is no secret that during the last years of his life King was deeply disappointed in the failure of the larger community to respond to his moral vision.

CHAPTER

6

GROWING DOWN

But yet I wonder if they did the crimes
Because most bad niggers would have left
   bodies (hundreds!) in a *line!*
But yet they escaped but without any *hate.*
Now they are caught;
Back their bodies have been brought.
Now the death chair's fire will shine.
It has been said by many signifying niggers
That the move was a class act, a work of art.
As always, there's the other hand,
Saying they should have blowed the system
apart!

—Charles Satchell
in Dance 1987

'Tis all in pieces, all cohaerence gone;
All just supply, and all Relation:
Prince, Subject, Father, Sonne, are things
   forgot,
For every man alone thinkes he hath got
For to be a Phoenix, and that then can bee
None of that kinde, of which he is, but hee.

—John Donne
in Bellah 1985

What do the continuing legacy of the black bad man and a seventeenth-century quote from John Donne have in common? The black man represents the epitome of individualism. John Donne laments such individualism and the lack of community and tradition in 1611, at the very beginning of the modern era. His views are used by Robert Bellah to describe the extreme individualism of contemporary American society.

From the slaves' Br'er Rabbit and Slave John to the more recent Great MacDaddy, John Henry, Railroad Bill, Dolemite, Shine, and Stackolee, the "bad nigger" or black "bad man" tradition is characterized by the absolute rejection of established authority figures. Through the tales and toasts we have surveyed in this work, they are celebrated for such largely negative actions as stealing, killing, fighting, gambling, pimping, and seducing. More modern versions are especially violent and tough, continuing their defiance whether in jail or hell or the briar patch. Moreover, the action is always carried out with great "style."

Daryl Dance has documented the continuing vitality of this tradition in *Long Gone.* On 31 May 1984, six condemned men at the Mecklenburg Correctional Center in Boydton, Virginia, carried out a bold escape from Death Row. Although the notorious Briley brothers and their cohorts were soon captured, the break inspired an evolving legend reminiscent of the bad man tradition.

Why are such negative figures so popular in the black community? Dance suggests that the most attractive feature of such characters is their rejection of authority and values that do not respect and value blacks. In addition, the actions of the bad men enable blacks to vicariously express the hostility and aggressiveness that they must normally repress. For teenage gangs and some adolescent groups, such figures serve as models for emulation, especially in their final attribute—their style. From the way they walk, to what they wear, to the way they interact with women and men, style is paramount (Dance 1987, 144–45).

Does this style-suffused mode of behavior offer a constructive alternative to mainstream values? Our analysis of the "blues" and the black bad man indicates that it does not. What it does offer, however, is survival and self-respect. It establishes visibility and identity by opposing values that attack the core of black existence. Thus the epitome of selfish individualism, the "bad nigger" cannot be understood apart from his cultural roots in the community. Moreover, he performs a community function in rejecting invisibility and asserting his identity and power.

What significance does the black style have for the mainstream society? As the quote from Dance indicates, the Mecklenburg escapees could have left a trail of bodies but chose not to. Some said they should have blown the system apart, but instead they escaped and returned without hate—"a class act, a work of art." This refusal to blow the system apart and lack of hate reflect a vision found in our discussion of the black church and black protest leaders. The ability of blacks to combine individualism and community as well as the sacred and secular is a hallmark of black politics and distinguishes it from mainstream politics.

THE INDIVIDUAL AND CULTURAL FRAGMENTATION

Shortly after his death in 1987, mythologist Joseph Campbell's work enjoyed a remarkable resurgence. His forty-year-old classic *Hero with a Thousand Faces* skyrocketed to the best seller list as did the published transcripts of his acclaimed PBS series on "The Power of Myth." Not only were people reading

Campbell but they were joining discussion groups to discuss his ideas. Modern interpretations of religious teaching, like Martin Scoresese's film *The Last Temptation of Christ*, have served to heighten the debate over the meaning of faith and tradition.

The guiding idea of Campbell's work was the search for the commonality of themes in world myths. He believed that myth and ritual bind society and the individual together by (a) opening the world to the dimension of mystery, (b) providing a cosmological foundation, (c) supporting and validating a certain social order, and (d) providing the basis for all education. In fact, Campbell's views provided the impetus for the most popular artistic myth of the seventies, the *Star Wars* epics (ibid.).

Recent sociological accounts of the state of American society help explain the popularity of Campbell and such epics as *Star Wars*. Our John Donne quotation is taken from Robert Bellah et al., *Habits of the Heart*. In their five-year study of various American communities (blacks were not included), Bellah and his colleagues found that an extreme reliance on individualism had caused many Americans to lose the language necessary to make moral sense of their lives. The fragmentation of intellectual culture has been caused by the disciplinary boundaries of modern science. The dominance of material ambition and sensationalism in popular culture, especially television and other mass media, makes a virtue of lacking all qualitative distinctions (Bellah 1985, 279–81).

If modernity is the culture of separation, says Bellah, we have little hope of finding meaning and coherence in our lives. There are, however, communities of memory which can give qualitative meaning to the living of life:

> we have never been, and still are not, a collection of private individuals who, except for a conscious contract to create a minimal government, have nothing in common. Our lives make sense in a thousand ways, most of which we are unaware of, because of traditions that are centuries, in not millennia, old. It is these traditions that help us to know that it does make a difference who we are and how we treat one another. (Bellah 1985, 282)

The idealized small town is a metaphor reflecting just such a yearning for meaning and coherence.

Richard Merelman reminds us of three such traditional cultures that have at one time or another given Americans coherence and direction. The earliest coherent vision of America as a cultural entity, states Merelman, was that of the Puritan fathers of New England. The vision combined a sense of destiny (jeremiad) with a sense of obligation to others. According to Merelman, the Puritan vision ultimately declined because its doctrine of voluntary consent laid the groundwork for the separation of church from state.

A more modern cultural vision of the United States is the democratic vision. If the Puritan vision laid the groundwork for civic religion, the democratic vision of the "Founding Fathers" legitimized participation and tolerance. The notion of consent builds a sense of trust in government, and groups that trust government feel that they can demand that government take an active role in improving society. Thus, the notion of individual consent can lead to increased government power. In short, trust permits people to join together in collective enterprises. Yet, says Merelman, the democratic vision has declined since World War II due to its failure to produce methods of organizing the public effectively through issue coalitions or political parties.

Finally, Merelman contends that an academic class vision of American life rose in the late sixties to explain the group conflict endemic to American life. This vision, however, soon faded in the face of an ideological superstructure that occupied a status at least equal to that of the economic base. In fact, it is the newer institutions of education, the mass media, and advertising that Merelman sees as creating an unusually extreme individualism among Americans (Merelman 1984, chapter 1).

The decline in these three visions of America has resulted in what Merelman calls "loosely bounded culture." While individualists might prefer such a culture, it lacks the meaning or stimulus to enable Americans to confront the massive, hierarchical political and economic structures that dominate their lives. Merelman prefers to see culture as a set of ideas which may empower the individual *against* social constraints.

We have been arguing throughout this work that black culture has empowered blacks to survive oppression and promote a community of interests. It has provided a social vision based on the integration of traditional elements of both black and white culture and as such has something to offer to the wider society. Unfortunately, this vision has been obscured rather than clarified by the rise of a black neoconservatism dominated by extreme individualism.

THE ISOLATION OF BLACK NEOCONSERVATIVES

Early in this century, Howard University Dean Kelly Miller reported that "[w]hen a distinguished Russian was informed that some American Negroes are radical and some conservative, he could not restrain his laughter. The idea of conservative Negroes was more than the Cossack's risibilities could endure. 'What on earth,' he exclaimed with astonishment, 'have they to conserve?' " (Miller 1968, 25). An objective of black institutions like Howard and much of the modern black studies movement has been to answer the Russian's question. Yet, ironically, the call for a return to basics led by white and black neoconservatives has opposed black studies and once again demonstrated the invisibility of black culture in mainstream academic circles.

Much of the current concern over "core curricula" stems from the belief that students are supposed to acquire a general sense of the world and their place in it. Today's universities, it is argued, more resemble cafeterias than libraries where "Great Books" are studied. Such views have made academic superstars out of professors like Allan Bloom and D. D. Hirsch.

Bloom's *The Closing of the American Mind* looks toward an old Europe and an even older Greece for his inspiration. While Bloom promotes what he labels "universal" values, Hirsch's *Cultural Literacy* proposes a more constricted vision, that of a "national culture." These visions, however, conflict with those promoted at the secondary level which stress technical knowledge and competition. For example, "A Nation at Risk," the report of the National Commission on Excellence in Education, cites the need to improve education so that the United States can maintain its competitive edge in the world marketplace. These authors look to Japan rather than Europe for inspiration.

This confusion of thought is prominent in the work of black neoconservatives. Black accommodationists like Booker T. Washington developed a number of black institutions and had programs for advancement—no matter how flawed.[1] Today's black neoconservatives lack a base in black institutions and only serve to legitimate the status quo. In this they differ even from the liberal black Republicans—James Cummings, Andrew Brimmer, Art Fletcher, Robert Browne, James Farmer, William T. Coleman, and in the Senate, Edward Brooke—who served under Presidents Nixon and Ford. These black Republicans generally sought to support affirmative action programs, civil rights legislation, and federal assistance to black colleges and black-owned businesses. They were, in short, able to combine a sense of individualism with a sense of group identity and government responsibility.

Today's black neoconservatives properly belong to the right wing of the Republican party and have severed ties with almost all black institutions. They can generally be placed in three categories: academics, government or party bureaucrats, and business executives. The best known among the academics are economists Thomas Sowell and Walter Williams, political scientist Martin Kilson, educator/religious leader Nathan Wright, Jr., Robert Woodson of the American Heritage Institute, and J. A. Y. Parker, president of the Lincoln Institute and Educational Foundation. Among the government and party officials are Thelma Duggin, Melvin Bradley, Thaddeus Garret, Clarence Pendleton, Jr., Henry Lucas, Jr., and Samuel Pierce. Black neoconservatives in the business community include Wendell Willkie Gunn, Gloria E. A. Toote, William Pickard, Arthur McZier, Constance Newman, Abraham Venable, Fred Blac, Cyrus Johnson, Philip J. Davis, and John Miller.

Manning Marable asserts that these "corporate Black Reaganites are even more dangerous than Sowell, because their blatant and vigorous support for conservative public policies is rooted not in any ideological commitment, but is grounded purely in their own vicious desire for money and their hunger for power" (Marable 1982, 175). Marable's perspective would seem to be reinforced by George Davis and Glegg Watson who write, in *Black Life in Corporate America,* that corporate America created for the first time in history large numbers of black people who "allowed the making of cash to determine their primary relationships to most of the people they knew. For black people there had always been some more important reasons for their relationships—fun, kinship, love, spiritual closeness, history. Now they were in the mainstream" (1982, 100).

Unlike the Washingtonian black entrepeneur working to establish a trade in the black community, the new corporate black is divorced from community life. However, most corporate blacks admit, according to Davis and Watson, that they are in corporations "because civil rights groups and the federal government pressured their companies into giving blacks a chance but all felt qualified, often over-qualified" (ibid., 40). Black managers (who number 4 to 5 percent of the total workforce) had more difficulty in carrying out their duties because the black life style is further from the corporate norm than the white life style. In addition, say Davis and Watson, "there was a great deal of *anomie,* a condition resulting from the breakdown of traditional values and norms of an individual who cannot or does not want to assimilate the values of a new, more complex and often inhospitable environment" (ibid., 40–41). When they did assimilate those values, there was a greater estrangement between them and their families and communities. This new generation of black managers is contrasted with the black corporate pioneers of the forties and fifties who "were social worker types conditioned by our parents to racial service and responsibility and not to get out there and do everything we could to make a dollar" (ibid., 21).

Unlike their corporate colleagues, the "ideological" or "academic" black conservatives appear unwilling to credit the liberal programs of the past for having any positive effect. In fact, the expansion of welfare programs is seen as a cause for the deterioration of black culture, especially the black family. Other specific issues black neoconservatives are concerned with include education, affirmative action, and minimum wage. On all of these issues, the position of black neoconservatives runs counter to black public opinion.

A recent poll conducted for *Time* magazine revealed that 59 percent of blacks thought blacks lacked equal opportunity in education, 62 percent supported affirmative action in employment, and 71 percent believed blacks lacked equal opportunity in employment. The comparable figures for whites were 24 percent, 32 percent, and 37 percent. An overwhelming 90 percent of blacks polled felt that the federal government should do more to promote equality in housing, education, and employment, while just slightly more than 50 percent of whites wanted more federal intervention (*Time,* 2 February 1987, 21).

Other polls with larger black survey populations indicate a 40 to 50 percent gap in the views of whites and blacks on the question of federal interventions (Schuman et al. 1985; Hamilton 1982; Welch and Combs 1985). Among ten leadership groups examined by Sidney Verba and Gary R. Orren, only blacks rated equality near the top as a national priority.[2] These studies support Martin Luther King's contention quoted at the beginning of this work that black and white Americans have different definitions of equality or at least attach different priorities to achieving it.

Yet the gap between blacks and whites on racial issues does not necessarily mean there is no common ground on nonracial matters. In his well-known work on the Harlem Renaissance, entitled *The New Negro,* Alain Locke states that "for the present the Negro is radical on race matters, conservative on others, in other words, a 'forceful radical,' a social protestant rather than a genuine radical" (Locke 1925, 11). Modern survey data would at least confirm that Afro-Americans are closer to the mainstream on nonracial issues, if not conservative. A 1972–1974 National Black Survey, for example, reveals that 43 percent of black voters and 50 percent of black nonvoters identified themselves as liberal on nonracial matters. On racial matters, however, the figures rose sharply to 85 percent and 90 percent respectively (Walton 1985, 32–33).

By focusing on issues of racial policy, broadly defined, black neoconservatives have isolated themselves from the traditional views of the black community. In failing to find anything worth conserving in black culture, they have ignored the very social issues on which a true black conservatism might rest. Black views on these issues are often linked to black religious fundamentalism. For example, Richard Seltzer and Robert C. Smith find that only on the issue of school prayer are blacks more conservative than whites.[3] Charles Hamilton lists a whole series of social issues on which blacks and whites share a conservative perspective. They include opposition to the legalization of marijuana, the condemnation of extramarital sex relations, tougher penalties for law violators, a belief that homosexuality is wrong, and the rejection of legal abortions. Hamilton notes that while blacks want the courts to be tougher on criminals, less than a majority favor the death penalty because of its disproportionate use against blacks and the poor (Hamilton 1982, 131–32). Thus, blacks' views on social issues are mediated by their belief in the fairness and equality of policy implementation.

REVERSING THE MORAL DILEMMA

Although the lack of black folk roots has meant that black neoconservatives have been isolated from black public opinion on policy issues, they have had some success in redefining the moral locus of some policy questions. Aligned with such white neoconservative scholars as Charles Murray, they have attempted to "blame the victim" by reviving the culture-of-poverty thesis. Murray's 1984 book *Losing Ground,* for example, examines the failures of the welfare system from the viewpoint of the "white popular wisdom." While Murray acknowledges that the majority of AFDC (Aid for Dependent Children) recipients are white, his argument for dismantling this federal program is based solely on the stereotypical black welfare mother. His argument assumes the tone of a moral crusade as he claims that "numbers (of babies) were not the issue; rather it was the notion of subsidizing a lifestyle that grated so harshly on the values held by consensus of white, middle-class Americans" (p. 19). Thus in the name of "white popular wisdom," Murray recommends a policy that will punish unrepentant blacks. The policy is presented as growing out of a con- cern for the debilitating consequences of the welfare system on the in- dependence of blacks. Murray's work received the enthusiastic endorsement of President Reagan.

Black neoconservatives like Orlando Patterson and Glenn Loury have also represented their policy positions as springing from similar concerns. In 1973, Patterson presented the choice for Black Americans as being between two basic types of moral systems: determinism and self-determinism or moral autonomy.[4] Furthermore, he asserts that "it seems incontestable that modern American society has a moral basis that is essentially autonomous" (1973, 43). The "moral crisis" for black Americans, according to Patterson is that while blacks would like to share this core value of individual moral responsibility for one's status, the most strategically useful moral system is determinism.

Empirical data on public attitudes concerning racial difference present a more complex picture. The ethic of individualism or self-reliance is certainly linked to conservatism on policy issues concerning race. However, Paul Sniderman and Michael Hagen point out that the individualist perspective must compete with those of progressives, fundamentalists, and historicists. Moreover, such a perspective is more characteristic of the working class than middle or upper classes. Finally, they note that individualism has historically stood for nonconformity as well as self-reliance (1985).

In his study of the San Francisco Bay area, Richard Apostle states that individualistic thinking about race constitutes a total of 39 percent of those examined. Although individualistic thinking has gained strength at the expense of a decline in genetic attitudes, the modern modes of environmentalists and environmental-radicals are gaining supporters, according to Apostle.

Having challenged Patterson's assumption that the individualistic ethic is so dominant that it must be accepted by blacks, we turn to the moral crisis he presents for the black community. While stating that black Americans have largely failed to grasp the existence of this dilemma, he does recognize that black fundamentalist religion has offered "the opportunity for the realization of personal responsibility which the Protestant version of the creed offers" (1973, 60). However, says Patterson, there are two major disadvantages which limit its scope as a medium of moral transformation. First, this religious transformation only marginally and sporadically permeates secular life. Second, the role of Christianity is declining rapidly among the younger urban generation. He doubts that a combined (sacred-secular) approach to moral transformation such as that of Jesse Jackson can work.

More recently, Glenn Loury has joined Patterson in arguing that blacks must "distinguish between the fault which may be attributed to racism as a cause of the black condition, and the responsibility for relieving that condition" (1985,

11). Loury places the responsibility for relief squarely on the shoulders of the black middle class who have benefited disproportionately from "liberal guilt" (this assertion seems to counter Patterson's assertion of the dominance of the individualist ethic among whites). He states that it is "beyond dispute that many of the problems of contemporary black American life lie outside the reach of effective government action" (1985, 10). Only blacks, especially the middle class, can effectively provide moral leadership for their people, says Loury.

The views of Patterson and Loury are part of a wider ideological effort launched by conservatives to reclaim moral hegemony for their values. This authority remained dominant from the development of white supremacy as a positive good in the 1820s and 1830s through the genetic arguments that peaked with World War I. Modern social science, led by anthropology, began to challenge the values embodied in white supremacy and culminated in the liberal guilt of the sixties. During the seventies the moral higher ground captured by King and the civil rights movement was gradually lost over such divisive issues as busing and affirmative action and the factionalization of support. The victory was completed with Ronald Reagan in 1980, who proclaimed the individualist ethic and called for a return to "old fashioned" (pre–civil rights) American values. However, the call for a minimalist state and moral autonomy poses a number of dilemmas for black conservatives.

For example, Patterson argues that black Americans must explain their failure to achieve. To argue that the minimal state provides the best opportunity for whites is one thing, but to make the same argument for a subordinated minority puts a special burden on black neoconservatives. They contend that in a free market, racial discimination is not a decisive cause of black subordination, yet they admit that markets have rarely been free. Moreover, they focus on employer discrimination to the exclusion of the tendency of the public to discriminate (Boxill 1984).

If black neoconservatives accept racism as a cause of black inequality and loss of self-esteem, then it is logically inconsistent for them to oppose compensation for blacks in the form of affirmative action. Once the cause is agreed upon, even the most advantaged of blacks is entitled to some degree of assistance. To reduce such questions as school segregation to test scores, as Sowell does, ignores the moral or self-esteem issue (Boxill 1984).

By separating the sacred (morally autonomous) perspective of the black church from everyday black secularism and by separating black middle-class values from black lower-class values, neoconservatives have attempted to redefine Myrdal's moral dilemma. Instead of the crisis in values facing white Americans whose behavior does not reflect the American Creed, it is now the black middle class—who have benefited from the American Creed—who must confront the value crisis of the black underclass. Wider society, according to the neoconservatives, is absolved of any responsibility for their lack of progress.

This moral segregation (as King might call it) has a precedent in the immediate post–Civil War period.[5] As mentioned earlier, V. P. Franklin points out that racial oppression, not religion, was the central defining element of black existence. There was not a dramatic shift from a sacred to a secular worldview, because the material conditions of a majority of blacks did not significantly change over the short run. This does not deny the fact that new possibilities were available as a goal and were attained by some.

COMMUNITY, COLONY, AND CULTURE

The growth of the black middle class in the 1970s and the rise of a black neoconservative elite which places sole moral responsibility for black progress in the hands of this middle class are best understood from a colonial perspective.[6] That is, of the major theoretical explanations of race relations and social change in the United States since the Civil War, the internal colony model offers the most comprehensive and heuristic treatment. Although various elements of such an approach have existed for over fifty years, it was the rise of black power and black consciousness in the sixties that stimulated its more complete development. Still, this model has some conceptual and definitional problems with culture.

As early as 1929, Ralph Bunche—who at that point considered himself to the left of Dubois—suggested that the organization of Negro society resembled a colony. In a critical analysis of "Marxism and the Negro Question," Bunche saw the development of class consciousness among blacks flowing naturally from rural to urban migration. In hindsight we know that this development of a class-conscious Negro proletariat did not occur. One notes, for example, the relative absence of folk songs extolling the virtues of black workers. Bunche might more easily have seen the obstacles to such a development had he focused more on the cultural and ideological response of blacks to urbanization and less on its economic consequences.

His economic focus led him to view southern blacks as a subject caste comparable to those of India.[7] He viewed this status as a pre-capitalist relic of the failure of Reconstruction to fully integrate blacks. Their feudalistic status produced for the land owner a profitable situation similar to colonial exploitation. The liberation of blacks from caste subjugation was the only uncompleted task of bourgeois democracy and in that respect was again similar to the liberation of subject colonies. However, said Bunche, bourgeois democracy was not capable of granting economic democracy, which could come only through the overthrow of capitalist democracy (a dialectical contradiction).

While Bunche recognized "the brilliant role of the Negro intellectual in the post-war 'renascence'" and gave the Negro petty bourgeoisie a more significant and progressive social role than the white bourgeoisie, he rejected the notion that blacks are a colonial people or a national minority. Moreover, "the process of class differentiation among the Negro people lays the basis for the liberation of the Negro masses from the influence of the white bourgeoisie (transmitted through the Negro bourgeoisie)" and, "for the achievement of the hegemony of the proletariat in the struggle for Negro emancipation" (Bunche 1929, 16). Thus, though he recognized the hegemonic role of bourgeois ideology in terms of race prejudice, Bunche made it clear that caste emancipation cannot come as a result of any purely racial movement.

Bunche's concept of caste—a concept shared with his colleague and friend Gunnar Myrdal—implied the acceptance of a consensual moral code replete with mutual religious and social obligations that we have argued has no firm base in historic reality. While Bunche does not go as far as Myrdal and Kenneth Clark (who uses the colonial analogy) in rejecting black culture as pathological, neither could he see it as a valid response to white hegemony. However, as we shall see, he was not alone in this failure.

The publication of Stokely Carmichael and Charles Hamilton's *Black Power* in 1967 marks the first elaboration of the colonial thesis. The failure of the interracial civil rights movement to bring about significant economic change, the violence of the late sixties, and the development of black power and Pan-African movements increased the popularity of the internal colony model. Carmichael and Hamilton's work was extended by that of Robert Allen, William Tabb, and Robert Blauner. While these works are not identical in their approach, they do share a number of basic similarities.

Like the conventional colony, the black colony in the United States is characterized by political powerlessness, economic dependence, and social isolation. Black communities are not self-supporting, and they lack resources for internal development. Having been stripped of their cultural heritage and socialized to the values of the colonial power, ghetto residents exhibit a subject mentality. They are often guided by a neo-colonial black elite which answers to the dominant white elite. Thus, according to the internal colony model, black Americans represent a distinct and subject people. This assertion has significance for theories that view race from both left and right perspectives.

THE AFRICAN PERSPECTIVE

African leaders like Amilcar Cabral—in defending African nationalism—have challenged the European model of history on which Marxist analysis is based:

> In the formation and development of individual or collective identity, the social condition is an objective agent, arising from economic, political, social and cultural aspects which are characteristic of the growth and history of the society in question. If one argues that the economic aspect is fundamental one can assert that identity is in a certain sense the expression of an economic

reality. This reality, whatever the geographical context and the path of development of the society, is defined by the level of productive forces (the relationship between man and nature) and by the means of production (the relations between men and between classes within this society). But if one accepts that culture is a dynamic synthesis of the material and spiritual condition of the society and expresses relationship both between man and nature and between the different classes within a society, one can assert that identity is at the individual and collective level and beyond the economic condition, the expression of culture. (Cabral 1973, 65–66)

While it is clear that Cabral is concerned with emphasizing the difference between the African bourgeoisie and the European bourgeoisie, his reconciliation of class and culture is significant for Afro-Americans.[8]

Sekou Toure goes so far as to declare that "culture is at a given time a social process, an infrastructure" (Toure 1974, 69). Since capitalism cannot stimulate spiritual culture,

[r]esistance, and then the offensive, will be organized first of all, in the cultural field. Colonized man must first recollect himself and critically analyze the results of the influences to which he was subjected by the invader, which are reflected in his behavior, his way of thinking and acting, his conception of the world and society, and his way of assessing the values created by his own people. (Toure 1974, 63)

Culture, for Toure, then represents an instrument of liberation and the first stage of consciousness.

In comparing black power to European ideologies, Richard Rubenstein puts this phenomenon in an American context. "Whereas European ideologies proceed from a philosophy of history to a vision of social transformation," says Rubenstein, "American ideologies more often proceed from a sense of group identity to a vision of independence" (Rubenstein 1970, 39). In other words, because of the legacy of racism and imperialism, third world ideologies tend to concentrate on defining the group, i.e., self-discovery, rather than defining their vision of a new society.

Robert Blauner states that racist oppression attacks selfhood more directly and thoroughly than does class oppression. Although both types of oppression interact, they have diverse consequences for group formation, for the salience of identities based upon them, and for individual and group modes of adaptation and resistance. According to Blauner, "class exploitation does not per se stimulate ethnic and national cultures and liberation movements; colonialism and domestic racism do" (Blauner 1972, 146). Blauner's work supports Albert Memmi's contention that the colonized—being oppressed as a group—must necessarily adopt a national and ethnic form of liberation. Moreover, Memmi adds that even the leftist colonizer will be excluded from this struggle because it is easier to commit "class suicide" than "cultural suicide" (Memmi 1965, 39).

Colonial theory helps explain the pursuit of a distinct African identity. The founders of the Philosophy of Negritude and those Africans who followed the ideas of Father Placide Tempel, the Belgian missionary who wrote *Bantu Philosophy*, were mainly concerned with demonstrating to a European audience that a truly African culture existed. "It was inevitable," says Paulin Hountonji, "that they should have ended up by inventing, as a foil to European philosophy, an African 'philosophy' concocted from extra-philosophical material consisting of tales, legends, dynastic poems, etc. . . . to derive from them what they could not, cannot and, will never yield: a genuine philosophy" (July 1987, 225).

Modern African critics of an "African philosophy" have embraced the tenets of western science and thought because they realize that African nations needed to be scientifically and technologically advanced to be truly independent. While these African philosophers did not want to concede the superiority of western civilization, they could not accept the assertion by numerous African humanists that reaffirmation of indigenous civilizations was an essential prerequisite to cultural emancipation from Europe. According to Robert July, a possible solution to the dilemma was offered by an African architect who conceded that there could be no going back to traditional technologies. "What had gone wrong," he contended, "was not the utilization of high technology but the unreflecting wholesale import of machines designed for other places and other needs, and often at costs beyond limited African budgets" (July 1987, 232). The solution was to adapt the best technology to the African condition, often through the use of an African design.

Of course, the problem of introducing high technology into local custom and tradition is more complex than the design of a machine or building. The large, impersonal westernized cities, for example, have created an impersonal ambience that erodes loyalties and breeds exploitation.[9] There is no trust in government, which is often viewed as something foreign, a linear descendant of the old colonial regime to be cheated. By contrast, the traditional village breeds an entirely different sense of civic responsibility. Privileges come with duties and everyone is responsible—everyone cares.

THE AFRO-AMERICAN PERSPECTIVE

The situation of Afro-Americans clearly differs from that facing Africans. Given their long history of interaction with whites, Afro-Americans have readily absorbed notions of scientific and technological progress. Moreover, they have participated in and need government to further group goals. At the same time their failure to be fully included has given them a sense of group cohesion and identity lacking in many white Americans.

The peculiar salience of racial and ethnic politics in the United States as compared to class has recently been examined by Ira Katznelson. He contends that as early as the 1830s and 1840s as places of work and residence were separated, an autonomous working-class culture developed. This culture defined residence or community problems on a racial-ethnic basis while viewing work problems from a class perspective.

By excluding blacks from traditional community (i.e. machine) politics, whites forced blacks to confront urban issues in new, unconventional ways. Black nationalism, as an ideological response to white exclusion and uneven economic development, placed these concerns under the rubric of internal colonialism, thus moving the conflict from the isolated community level to a wider scope. While black power or community control did not raise basic questions concerning monopoly capital, the holistic worldview of black nationalism did produce demands that in two respects were radically different from traditional urban politics.

In the first place, says Katznelson, blacks did not respect traditional boundaries between issues. School, welfare, police, and housing issues were seen as aspects of a total or colonial condition, which made it much more difficult for authorities to manage or supply piecemeal solutions. Second, these policy areas were joined with questions of government and economic redistribution rather than being viewed as simple matters of patronage and services (Katznelson 1981, 120–21). Thus, whether directly or indirectly, black demands for community control challenged the prevailing political economy because they could not be met at the urban level alone.

The institutional innovation of decentralization was used to thwart these radical demands. Among the reasons behind the blunting of social change were, says Katznelson, the focus on territorial aspects of community control, the emphasis on linkages between government and the residence community, and the inability of black nationalism to directly address political economy on a macroanalytic scale. But above all else, states Katznelson, "The resilience of the political culture of the traditional urban system and its close resemblance to the ethos of black protest made it very hard for blacks to get a confirming response to the global features of their insurgency from the larger society and tended to dissolve the nationalist thrust under the mimetic policy responses of local government" (Katznelson 1981, 177). In short, government authorities were able to blunt radical insurgency by devising new institutions at the local level that allowed limited black participation but relied on traditional ethnic-racial divisions to prevent radical change.

The colonial model has the advantage of symbolically linking Afro-American and third world struggles. We have seen that this linkage is important in establishing Afro-American identity and promoting foreign policy views that suport the overthrow of colonialism and imperialism. This support can be grounded in the American Revolution, although it is a tradition often overlooked in modern America.

Beyond symbolism, colonial theory, by focusing on structural discrimination, moves toward the cause of inequality rather than the result. It also facilitates comparative analysis across national boundaries. Thus, we can see the distinctions between modernizing African nations and Afro-Americans in an advanced, technological society.

Unlike deficiency theories, which tend to place the blame on the inherent characteristics of the minority group itself, the colonized-people approach points out the conflictual nature of the political system and the inequality of resources. From this perspective, the difference between Afro-Americans and white ethnic groups becomes clearer.

Yet, as we have seen, other ethnic groups can assert their own identity and exploit the differences to the detriment of blacks. Instead of using the "chosen people" metaphor for inclusion, they use it for exclusion. This has led social scientists to decry the use of such primitive ties as race and religion.

The real problem, however, is not the assertion of identity. It is only in relationship with others that we find meaning in life and learn how to live. The answer lies in balancing the forces of ascription or descent with those of achievement or consent. We have argued that the balance has swung too far in the direction of possessive individualism to give meaning and purpose to our daily lives and our life as a nation. Allan Bloom's old Europe and ancient Greece lack the modern metaphors to give us a collective social vision. Joseph Campbell's search for the commonality in world myths and Jesse Jackson's search for common ground are part of the same struggle to find the ties that bind us together as a world community and as a national community.

This work has sought to provide an introduction to the way in which mass or folk culture has been used as a mechanism for survival and an instrument for liberation. Our examination of several hundred folktales, proverbs, songs, and sermons sought to provide an insight on the ways in which folk culture mediates political behavior. We found that the messages being communicated are often complex and at times contradictory. However, certain themes continually re-emerge. Moreover, the medium is as often as important as the message. Style is in itself a statement of identity and an assertion of freedom.

Black politics, then, may be distinguished from a more encompassing American politics by its inclusion of a wider variety of political expression and demand, by its emphasis on identity and self-respect which crosses class lines, by its dependence on rhetoric and charisma, and by its rootedness in a black church tradition that blends sacred and secular vision. It is tied inexorably to American politics as a whole but is also linked to the struggles of oppressed groups worldwide. Its moral vision and international insight give it a transforming potential not found in mainstream American politics. (See Diagram 1.)

Yet black politics also contains seeds of reconciliation and synthesis. The novels of two ethnic Americans, one black and one Jewish, provide examples

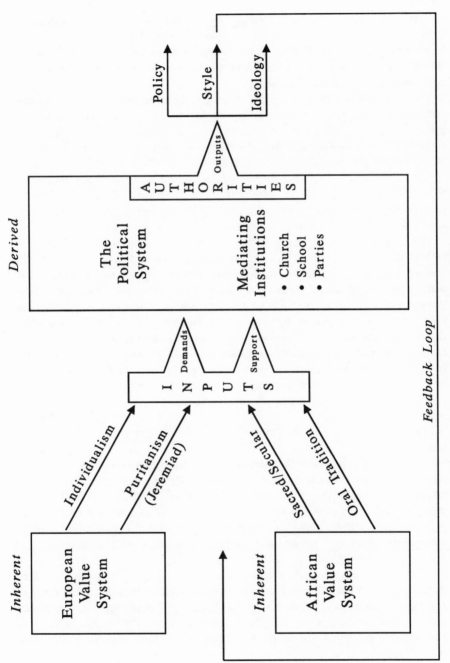

Diagram 1. A Systems-Process Model of Black Politics

of this potential. James Weldon Johnson's *Autobiography of an Ex-Colored Man* and Abraham Cahan's *Autobiography of an American Jew* (later *The Rise of David Levinsky*) were written around the same time (1913–1917) and are similar in literary strategy. Both have protagonists who forsake the creative possibilities of their ethnic roots for successful though unfulfilling business careers. Yet in real life both authors took the opposite route from their fictional alter egos. According to Werner Sollars:

> Neither Cahan nor Johnson saw descent statistically as a force that American men could return or withdraw to. They knew that consent was here to stay. Their ideal vision was that of a synthesis of specific descent and cosmopolitan consent, a synthesis best expressed in musical metaphors. This harmonization of the descent and consent dimensions within one human being should lead to an existence in which success on American terms was to be realized artistically without compromising self-denials. Locating the tensions between consent and descent within the consciousness of one man—the unreliable narrator and protagonist—Johnson and Cahan cast the opposition in such a way that the figure of *the successful musician appears as a possible synthesis.* (Emphasis mine, Sollars 1986, 1973)

Notes

1. IDEOLOGY, POLITICS, AND CULTURE

1. A general definition of the American creed might include those beliefs embodied in the Bill of Rights, the preamble to the Constitution, and the Declaration of Independence. Among the rights most often cited are those of life, liberty, and the pursuit of happiness; property rights; the right of free speech and assembly; equality under law; and the principle of power deriving from the consent of the governed.

2. This definition is consistent with that of David Easton, *A Systems Analysis of Political Life* (New York: Wiley & Sons, 1965), 290 and Clifford Geertz, *The Interpretation of Cultures* (New York: Basic, 1973), 196. Note that Easton allows for partisan ideologies within a political community which do not necessarily challenge the legitimating ideology of that society. He would argue that much of what may be considered Afro-American ideology could be subsumed under the label of partisan ideology. However, our use of the term is more broad-based than that suggested by Easton.

3. Throughout this work we will discuss various works purporting to explain the behavioral differences of blacks in politics in regard to the white norm. Some of the more recent efforts on black political behavior include the following: Schley Lyons, "The Political Socialization of Ghetto Children," *Journal of Politics* 32 (May 1970), 258–304; David Schultz, *Coming Up Black* (Englewood Cliffs, N.J.: Prentice-Hall, 1969); Milton D. Morris and Carolyn Cove, "The Political Socialization of Black Youth," *Public Affairs Bulletin* (S.I.U., May–June 1972), 5; Edward S. Greenberg, "Children and Government," *Midwest Journal of Political Science* 10 (February 1966), 123–37; Edward S. Greenberg, "Orientations of Black and White Children to Political Authority Figures," *Social Science Quarterly* 51 (December 1970), 561–71; Herbert Hirsch and Lewis Donohew, "A Note on Negro-White Differences in Attitudes toward the Supreme Court," *Social Science Quarterly* 49, 3 (December 1968); Anthony Orum and Roberta Cohen, "The Development of Political Orientations among Black and White Children," *American Sociological Review* 38 (February 1973); A. H. Singham, "The Political Socialization of Marginal Groups," *International Journal of Comparative Sociology* 8 (September 1976); Charles Bullock and Harrell Rogers, *Black Political Attitudes* (Chicago: Markham, 1972); N. L. Danigelis, "Black Political Participation in the U.S.," *American Sociological Review* 43 (1978), 756–71, also "Theory of Black Political Participation in the U.S.," *Social Forces* 56 (1977), 31–47; Leslie Burl McLemore, "Toward a Theory of Black Politics: The Black and Ethnic Models Revisited," *Journal of Black Studies* 2 (1972), 323–31; Philip Miller, "The Impact of Organizational Activity on Black Political Participation," *Social Science Quarterly* 63 (1982), 83–98; Marvin E. Olsen, "Social and Political Participation of Blacks," *American Sociological Review* 35 (1970), 682–97; John C. Pierce et al., "Efficiency and Participation," *Journal of Black Studies* 2 (1973), 201–23; R. D. Shingles, "Black Consciousness and Political Participation," *American Political Science Review* 75, (1981), 76–91; Pauline Stone, "Ambition Theory and the Black Politician," *Western Political Quarterly* 33 (1980), 94–107; Paul Abramson, *Black Political Socialization* (New York: The Free Press, 1977).

4. For a detailed critique of works of this genre see chapter 3.

5. In discussing the power of stylistic mechanisms to trigger meaning, Geertz cites General Sherman's maxim that "war is hell" as an overexaggeration many would agree with. Yet in pre–World War II Japan, war was cited as "the father of creation and the mother of culture." Despite the differing historical contexts, Geertz believes Sherman's

vision of war was much closer to the truth than that of the Japanese. In short, the truth does not vary but the symbols we construct to grasp it do (Geertz 1973, 211–12).

6. A favorite example of ideological inconsistency in the mass population often occurs on questions of free speech. Quite often the vast majority of those polled indicate that they believe in free speech but reverse their position when asked if a Communist should have the right to lecture at a university. To cite such findings as ideological inconsistency removes the meanings concerned from their cultural context. The "founding fathers" themselves meant to exclude certain groups from the First Amendment and rightly assumed that others would understand the context in which such an objective law is written. Moreover, as Walter Rosenbaum indicates, attitudes as reflected in polls do not always translate into action. Members of an educated elite are much better equipped to hide their antidemocratic tendencies than the uneducated (Rosenbaum 1975, 150). This would account for much of the frustration felt by Martin Luther King in dealing with white liberals.

7. One should note that virtually all literary traditions emerge from oral sources such as Homer's *Odyssey* and *Iliad,* which were originally folksongs. For an excellent example of an African oral epic, see Daniel Biebuyck and Kahombo C. Mateene, eds., *The Mwindo Epic* (Berkeley: Univ. of California, 1971).

8. Adda Bozeman believes that nonliteracy makes it extremely difficult for the traditional African to separate thought from action. She believes that the traditional states were based on invisible but stable mythical subcultures (1976, 144). In modern Asian and African societies the traditional use of rhetoric and verbal deceit in statecraft make diplomacy with the West unpredictable (1971, 7).

Ali A. Mazrui contends that the failure of African languages to develop a technical component led to Africa being left behind scientifically. According to Mazrui it was the language and not the minds of Africans that could not stimulate new areas of reflection and analysis (1974, 87).

2. BLACK AND BLUE

1. Laura Carper has argued that one could easily make the same point about female-headed families in regard to Jews. She reviews family life in the East European Jewish shtetl as an example of depersonalized social science research (see Gutman 1976, 464–65). Glazer and Moynihan also tend to focus on Afro-American deviations even though four other ethnic groups are reviewed in their study.

2. Donald Crummey distinguishes between protest studies and resistance studies. Protest entails a higher degree of vocalization and assumes some common social and political order linking protesters and those to whom the protesters appeal. Resistance, on the other hand, expects no redress or grievances from within the system and often operates secretly. Thus radical black nationalists might appeal to traditional black values that separate them from whites while conservative black nationalists might seek out traditional black values that unite them with whites as equals (see Crummey 1986, 10).

3. An interesting example of folktale providing a "conservative" interpretation of male-female relationships is entitled "De Ways of De Wimmens." The beginning of the tale pictures Adam and Eve engaged in a tremendous fight in the Garden of Eden. The battle has no victor because the Lord had created both with equal strength. Adam seeks out the Lord and asks for superior strength to overcome a new tactic Eve has learned from the devil—the weapon of tears. The Lord gives Adam new muscles and he proceeds to assert his physical authority over Eve. Eve returns to the devil for two new weapons that make her boss of all married men—the keys to the bedroom and the kitchen! (Langston Hughes and Arna Bontemps, eds., *The Book of Negro Folklore* (New York: Dodd, Mead & Co., 1966), 130–35). For a current literary treatment of this theme see Alice Walker's *The Color Purple.*

4. Dena Epstein states that the rise of black prejudice against secular music and dancing cannot be traced to Africa, where such distinctions between sacred and secular did not exist. "This is one case," she says, "where blacks appear to have been influenced by whites, for a prejudice against dancing can be documented among white evangelicals from the early 18th century" (1977, 208).

5. In a sense the rise of gospel music to fit the needs of Southern lower-class blacks moving to the urban North at the turn of this century parallels the "Great Awakening" movement in the eighteenth century. Both were a reaction to the staid psalmody and hymnody of the religious establishment. Of course, it is the "Second Awakening" in camp meetings that gives birth to the spiritual (see Southern 1971, 97). The music of middle-class blacks prior to the Civil War followed the "trite" and rather superficial music favored by white society during this period (ibid., 104).

6. C. Eric Lincoln has argued that the black cults and sects which arose in response to great black migrations during World War I actually served an integrative function. Since these groups were isolated, insulated, and politically non-involved, they retrieved and stabilized elements of the black community who were potentially miscontents (Lincoln in Gordon 1979, 171–75).

7. Mays's study suffers from a dubious separation of "classical" and "mass" literature. However, it is worth noting that beginning with the Harlem Renaissance and the Depression, there is a new willingness on the part of young creative writers and some social scientists like Frazier and Bunche to reveal the ugly side of black life. In a sense this willingness parallels the development of the blues. Of course, older race spokespersons such as DuBois, Kelly Miller, and Carter Woodson thought such works detracted from the case to be made for integration.

8. Despite the optimism Haralambos finds in soul music, a recent class analysis of black and white families pointed out that while both black and white marriages become more stable with a rise in class position, disruption rates in black marriages are uniformly far higher than in white marriages at all class levels. The author, Daniel Rossides, concludes "that black marriages bear not only class factors but also the legacy of slavery" (Daniel Rossides, *The American Class System* [Boston: Houghton Mifflin, 1978], 189).

9. The resolution of intragroup conflict is illustrated by the origins of "jazz." With the development of "Jim Crow" forcing blacks and Creoles together in New Orleans in 1894 and 1896 and a massive influx of foreign immigration, intense competition and striving for group identity occurred. The mixing of the styles of black musicians and Creole musicians created "jazz," which helped develop a sense of common cultural identity and uplift morale. Intragroup conflict was reduced as new dances emphasizing close contact were developed (see Wilson 1972, 56–59, also Southern 1971).

10. John S. Roberts states that "[I]n Africa music is not so much 'good' as 'effective,' that is, right for its purpose. A 'beautiful voice' in the European sense is an accident, not the main point . . . the criteria for choosing a singer are social, not musical" (Roberts 1972, 8). This would account for the frequency of "earthy" rather than "pretty" voices among blues singers.

11. Commenting on the individuality of the blues, John Lovell states that "[A]lthough an artistic device, the pronoun I appears as the lead element in hundreds of spirituals. The I of the blues frankly enlists the support of a sympathizing group. Since, regardless of their authorship, both are obviously folksongs, such a distinction can never stand" (Lovell 1972, 464). Lawrence Levine, however, attaches much more significance to the individuality of the blues, viewing it as acculturation to American individualism (Levine 1977).

12. The following account of the evolution of rap music relies heavily on David Cook's "The Story of Rap" prepared for *Afro-American Studies 5A,* University of California at Berkeley, 1985–86. As an art form rap music has probably peaked in the

black ghetto. With its widespread popularity among all classes—see the rap videos by the America's Cup Crew and the Chicago Bears—it has lost its uniqueness as a black cultural form. Even if a rapprochement between black rap and white rock has been reached with the collaboration of Run-DMC and Aerosmith on the hit "Walk This Way," as the *New York Times* (28 December 1986) claims, history tells us a new and uniquely black form will come to replace it.

3. AFRO-AMERICAN STYLE AND LOWER-CLASS BEHAVIOR

1. Philip Abbot suggests that an emphasis on leadership is a problem faced by all pluralists who confront the dilemma of creating a system of uniform laws for all society while placing one's supreme value on diversity. He cites Theodore Lowi's "anti-leadership system" of "juridical democracy" as one proposal for developing "citizens" rather than "followers." Lowi recommends studying social movements rather than groups as a method for stimulating social change. In fact, we have seen that black politics are especially prone to social movements, yet leadership remains a vital element. (See *Furious Fancies—American Political Thought in the Post-Liberal Era* [Westport, Conn.: Greenwood, 1980], 103–105.)

2. The dominant theoretical perspective in political science follows an ethnic model within a pluralist framework that treats blacks as an ethnic group. See Robert Dahl, *Who Governs?* (New Haven: Yale, 1961); Edward Banfield and James Q. Wilson, *City Politics* (Cambridge, Mass.: Harvard, 1966); and Nathan Glazer and Daniel P. Moynihan, *Beyond the Melting Pot* (Cambridge: MIT, 1963). For a view that challenges these positions with particular reference to Chicago, see Dianne Pinderhughes, *Race and Ethnicity in Chicago Politics* (Urbana: University of Illinois Press, 1987), and Marguerite Ross Barnett and James A. Hefner, eds., *Public Policy for the Black Community* (New York: Alfred, 1976).

3. In his "Through the Prism of Folklore: The Black Ethos in Slavery" (*Massachusetts Review,* Summer 1968), Sterling Stuckey attacks Genovese's view of slave stealing from the master as self-destructive. He argues that such actions increased the slave's self-respect and that "day to day resistance moved along meaningful rather than nihilistic lines" (pp. 431–32).

4. It is interesting to note that Abrahams, Jackson, and Levine do agree that the folk legend "Shine" represents a combination or mediation of the trickster and bad man. As such, he might better represent the prototype for the "superspade" of recent black films than the bad man.

5. H. Bruce Franklin relates that one referee of an academic journal insisted that Douglass's real moment of liberation was the intellectual act of writing his narrative rather than the use of brute strength and physical violence cited by Douglass himself. Franklin suggests that this academician, as well as Jean Genet in the introduction to George Jackson's *Soledad Brother* and Jean-Paul Sartre in the introduction to Fanon's *The Wretched of the Earth,* are examples of radically different outlooks on the phenomena discussed in the respective books.

6. Claude Brown in Samuel G. Freeman, "Violence against Blacks Spotlights Racial Strife," *New York Times,* 2 January 1987: Y 11. Manning Marable reports that more than 8 percent of all Afro-Americans are arrested every year (*How Capitalism Underdeveloped Black America* [Boston: South End Press, 1983], 127). Obviously the figure for inner-city black youth is much higher.

7. Significantly, Garvey, Malcolm X, and George Jackson share the belief of many more moderate black leaders (King, Kenneth Clark, Rustin) that the liberation of black America may ultimately lead to the liberation of white America.

8. While it is beyond the scope of this study to explore gender differences in Afro-American and African folklore, they are significant and should provide a rewarding

area of further study. For example, Afro-American folklore is replete with tales that emphasize distrust between males and females. See, for example, "Tad's Advice to His Son" and "Old Sister's Advice to Her Daughters" in Edward C. L. Adams, *Congaree Sketches* (Chapel Hill: University of North Carolina Press, 1927). Ralph A. Austen notes that African literature stresses the prostitute rather than the criminal as the threat to the social order (see Crummey, op. cit.). In Robert Farris Thompson's *Flash of the Spirit* (New York: Vintage, 1984), he notes that "[m]any riveranin goddesses are visualized as women with swords. The sword, together with the negative uses of the fan, may be said to form in part an image of what Judith Hoch-Smith calls 'radical yoruba female sexuality. . . . Witchcraft, in fact, militates against not only total male dominance but the threat of class formation and drastically unequal distribution of wealth'" (p. 74). In fact, says Austen, "the idiom which more specifically addresses the relationship of marginal figures to changes in authority and property rights is that of witchcraft" (p. 102).

4. JEREMIADS AND THE IDEOLOGICAL FUNCTIONS OF BLACK RELIGION

1. Timothy L. Smith states that blacks, unlike other American ethnic groups, used the chosen people metaphor to affirm their common humanity rather than their separateness. The favorite passage of whites was John 3:16 but for blacks it was Paul's announcement to the Athenians that God "made of one blood all nations of men for to dwell on the face of the earth"("Slavery and Theology," *Church History* 41, no. 4, December 1972).

2. Wilson J. Moses has given us the most complete treatment of the Afro-American jeremiad in *Black Messiahs and Uncle Toms* (University Park: Pennsylvania State University Press, 1982). David Howard-Pitney's article, "The Jeremiads of Frederick Douglass, Booker T. Washington, and W. E. B. DuBois and Changing Patterns of Black Messianic Rhetoric, 1841–1920," *Journal of American Ethnic History* 6, no. 1 (Fall 1986), is an excellent supplement to Moses. Moses contends that the use of jeremiad declined with the deaths of King and Malcolm X. However, the rise of Ronald Reagan, the Moral Majority, and Jesse Jackson make this conclusion suspect.

3. Coincidentally on the same day the Senate took up debate on the bill to make King's birthday a national holiday, Prime Minister Edward Seaga of Jamaica asked President Reagan to grant a full pardon to Marcus Garvey (Oakland *Tribune,* 18 October 1983).

4. Another major difference in Cone's theology as compared to King's is its nationalistic orientation. Molefi Kete Asante argues that King was himself standing between the apathetic and the nationalist (Asante 1980, 17). Cone, on the other hand, directly links true Christianity to the liberation of blacks. Yet Cone's theology has been challenged as too heavily dependent on European theological constructs, as is perhaps King's (see Long 1971, 54–65).

5. African theologian John Mbiti questions the ends of black theology once its immediate goal of liberation is reached: "[b]lack theology is deeply 'eschatological,' yet its eschatological hopes are not clearly defined" (Mbiti in Wilmore and Cone 1979, 479). Thus while King may be too concerned with religious ends, Cone may be too involved in political ends.

6. Several social scientists have argued that urban rebellions in the North are simply an expansion of protest tactics geared to the urban ghetto. Urban participants in such protests, as King noted in one case, felt they had won because they made whites pay attention to them (see Schuman and Hatchett 1974; Feagin and Hahn 1973).

7. While much of King's rhetoric, as well as that of his chief lieutenant in Chicago, Jesse Jackson, is integrationist, his own organization, SCLC, and its Chicago branch, Operation Breadbasket, are squarely rooted in the black community. Charles Hamilton

cites Operation Breadbasket's economic programs as an example of what black power advocates mean by community control (see Hamilton in Scott and Brockriede, 183; see also Barbara Reynolds 1975). Despite his best efforts at broadening its base, Jesse Jackson's Rainbow Coalition in 1984 was overwhelmingly black and supported by nationalists like Maulana Karenga and Louis Farrakhan.

5. CULTURAL POLITICS AND THE JACKSON CAMPAIGN

1. Barbara Reynolds, *Jesse Jackson: The Man, the Movement, the Myth* (Chicago: Nelson-Hall, 1975), 235.

2. Jesse L. Jackson, "The Candidate's Challenge," speech before the Democratic National Convention, San Francisco, 17 July 1984, 4.

3. Davis and I disagree on the order in which Jackson presents certain elements of his political sermon. Davis finds Jackson stumbling through a written speech and then abandoning the text to move into a traditional sermon. I was present for the speech and viewed some of the most effective moments coming early (with his apology to Jews) and late. The middle part with its data was flat by comparison. His introduction by various minorities and the closing song were also effective. Tears flowed freely throughout the audience.

4. Nancy Skelton, "Jackson Blames News Media for Outsider Status," *Oakland Tribune,* 20 March 1984; Tom Sherwood, "Jackson Says He's Hindered by Stereotypes," *Oakland Tribune,* 22 March 1984.

5. Reynolds, 100.

6. Ibid., 159.

7. Gerald L. Davis, *I Got the Word in Me and I Can Sing It, You Know* (Philadelphia: Univ. of Pennsylvania Press, 1985), 67–80.

The pioneering work of Henry H. Mitchell generally supports Davis's findings. However, Mitchell argues that a universal factor in the black sermon seems to be climatic material, yet he also stresses that the sermon must be fresh and immediately relevant like a jazz riff or gospel improvisation. See *Black Preaching* (New York: Harper & Row, 1979), 166, 202.

8. Georgia M. Swanson, in whose dissertation these first three speeches appear, finds many more messianic and sexist themes than this author. The speech to the youth conference dwells on the pitfalls of casual sex, largely, one supposes, because it is a major preoccupation of teenagers. See "Messiah or Manipulator? A Burkean Cluster Analysis of the Motivations Revealed in the Selected Speeches of the Reverend Jesse Louis Jackson," unpublished doctoral dissertation, Bowling Green State University, June 1982.

9. Jackson's tying of the collective self-respect and moral integrity of his campaign to the issue of fairness or justice is a potent traditional theme in Afro-American politics. While Reed argues that moral leadership has no categorical meaning in the political world, one cannot make that assertion with regard to black politics. Bernard R. Boxill, for example, states that Martin Luther King, Jr., appealed to America's conscience because he believed that everyone had the same conscience he had. But King, says Boxill, only assumed that, deep down, Americans agree on questions pertaining to the justice of law. See *Blacks and Social Justice,* 213.

10. Although the texts of two of Jackson's speeches do not contain any specific call for an audience reaction, much is lost in transferring black performance to the written page. Having heard Jackson on several occasions at Operation Breadbasket and most recently at the 1984 Democratic Convention, the author can attest to Jackson's emotional impact on both black and white audiences.

11. Harold A. Carter points out that King's 1963 March on Washington speech was preceded by King's 1957 "Prayer Pilgrimage" to Washington. King closed his remarks

that day with James Weldon Johnson's "Lift Every Voice and Sing." Carter considers this song—known as the Negro National Anthem—as a model prayer. See *The Prayer Tradition of Black People* (Valley Forge: Judson Press, 1976), 112–15. One should also note the shift in form between the 1957 prayer for national repentance and the 1963 call for a civil rights bill (sacred to secular).

12. The author randomly selected each fifth sermon in these two collections for examination. This totaled over forty sermons in the two collections that were analyzed. Most of Johnson's sermons were from the 1920s, and Brown's sermons were delivered during the 1930s, 1940s, and 1950s.

13. A few sermons drew on more than one biblical text. The breakdown is: New Testament, 56 citations; Old Testament, 41 citations.

14. Nan Bailey, et al., *The National Black Independent Political Party* (New York: Pathfinder, 1981).

15. William Schneider, "The Dividing Line between Delegates Is Age," *National Journal Convention Daily* 16 July 1984.

16. Maulana Karenga, "Jesse Jackson and the Presidential Campaign," *The Black Scholar* 15, no. 5 (September–October 1984).

17. Adolph L. Reed, Jr., *The Jesse Jackson Phenomenon* (New Haven: Yale, 1986), 1.

18. Ibid., 34.

19. V. P. Franklin, *Black Self-Determination* (Westport, Conn.: Lawrence Hill, 1984), 195–202.

20. Gerald Davis reports that the use of such sound devices as crescendo effects and repetition of key phrases are common in the traditional black sermon.

21. Before predominantly black audiences, Jackson's speeches were even more characteristic of black revival meetings. The author attended three Black Caucus meetings at the 1984 Democratic National Convention that were addressed by Jackson. In each instance he opened his remarks with a prayer and closed with the communal singing of a spiritual or gospel song.

22. Peter J. Paris notes "that one important locus of considerable social criticism in the black denominations was the women's organizations which often caused the offical denominational leaders more than a little consternation. Time and again the women kept specific issues of racial injustice alive that were otherwise concealed in the generalized rhetoric of those occupying the highest positions of power and authority" (*The Social Teaching of the Black Churches* [Philadelphia: Fortress Press, 1985], 80). Thus the relatively high electoral participation of black women may be seen as a continuation of traditional social activism in the black church.

23. Charles P. Henry, "Racial Factors in the 1982 California Gubernatorial Campaign," paper presented at the annual meeting of the Western Political Science Association, Seattle, March 1983.

24. Vietnam is the only foreign policy issue of recent decades seen as having high visibility and the potential for realignment. However, the two major parties took similar positions on Vietnam, and its realigning potential was not realized (see Scammon and Wattenberg 1971).

25. See, for example, Andrew Kopkind and Alexander Cockburn, "The Left, the Democrats and the Future," *The Nation* (July 21–28, 1984) and Miriam Quinones et al., "Women's Stake in the Rainbow," *The Black Scholar* 15, no. 5, (September–October 1984).

6. GROWING DOWN

1. Marable cites William Hooper Councill as the leading black conservative during the "Age of Washington." After the Civil War, Councill became a leading black Democrat in northern Alabama and president of the black segregated state school at Hunts-

ville. In 1873 he was secretary for the National Equal Rights Convention and in 1887 appealed his exclusion from a first-class railway car to the Interstate Commerce Commission. Alabama whites quickly retaliated by removing him at the school and he regained his position only after renouncing integration and promoting black docility. Councill was so morally bankrupt that even Booker T. Washington would not share a platform with him. (See Marable 1982, 173, 185–87; and Harlan 1972, 168–69.)

2. Verba and Orren report that six of the ten groups placed "equality for blacks" in the bottom three priority categories. The groups surveyed included business, farm, labor, intellectuals, media, Republicans, Democrats, blacks, feminists, and youth. See Sidney Verba and Gary R. Orren, *Equality in America* (Cambridge: Harvard Univ. Press, 1985), 121.

3. Seltzer and Smiths' data reveal that on issues either directly or indirectly related to race, blacks are more liberal than whites. These issues include crime control, the death penalty, gun control, school busing, government spending to improve race conditions, and segregated housing. However, on support of the Supreme Court's decision prohibiting school prayer, blacks are significantly more conservative than whites. Black Northerners are less conservative than black Southerners on this issue, but opposition includes all educational strata. See Richard Seltzer and Robert C. Smith, "Race and Ideology: A Research Note Measuring Liberalism and Conservatism in Black America," *Phylon* 46, no. 2 (Summer 1985), 98–105.

4. Thomas Sowell's *A Conflict of Vision* (New York: Morrow, 1987) expands this perspective to include most contemporary policy issues. The two conflicting perspectives at the root of policy debates, says Sowell, are those with constrained vision (original sin) and those with unconstrained vision (perfectability of man).

5. Orlando Patterson presents the same approach as Eugene Genovese in describing the moral problem created by slaves stealing from the master. For Patterson, "fine distinctions between degrees of enormity of crime are morally frivolous" and "there is the undeniable objection that to excuse one's actions on deterministic grounds while condemning similar actions on the part of one's oppressor on morally autonomous grounds is both ethically unacceptable and, of itself morally contemptible" (1973, 54).

6. These other approaches include the dominant perspectives of the caste model and the ethnic group model and the non-dominant perspective of the Marxist model. For an excellent discussion of all four approaches see Herman George, Jr., *American Race Relations Theory* (Lanham, MD: University Press of America, 1984). For an excellent synthesis of race and class perspectives, see Mario Barrera, *Race and Class in the Southwest* (Univ. of Notre Dame Press, 1979). For a comparative perspective on the development of intellectual paradigms, see August Meier and Elliott Rudwick, *Black History and the Historical Profession 1915–1980* (Urbana: Univ. of Illinois Press, 1986) and Gayraud S. Wilmore and James H. Cone, eds., *Black Theology: A Documentary History, 1966–1979* (Maryknoll, N.Y.: Orbis, 1979).

7. The comparison of caste relations in India to black relations in the pre-industrial South is often made but seldom critically analyzed. Herman George, Jr., has pointed out a basic problem facing caste advocates in explaining social change. Since traditional caste society rests on a system of mutual obligations and prerogatives that define all social interaction of castes and limits mobility to intra-caste improvements, social change must come as a result of external factors. Thus, when a caste advocate like Myrdal looks to a modern political economy to generate liberalizing changes, he is admitting the inability of pre-capitalist, agricultural, caste social principles to explain social change (George 1984, 183).

8. In his critique of the neo-Pan-Africanists, Henry Winston is careful to distinguish them as Garvey Pan-Africanists. DuBois's Pan-Africanism is regarded as acceptable since DuBois eventually joined the Communist party. However, Herbert Aptheker, a party

member and authority on DuBois, contends that DuBois joined the party on his own terms. He was not a Marxist or dialectical materialist, says Aptheker, but rather a "DuBoisite" (Aptheker, Spring 1984, class notes). Winston also argues that neo-Pan-Africanists "would have us accept as Black culture everything created by Blacks, without regard to its content" (Winston 1973, 39). He gives as an example the novels of Frank Yerby. Yet, most of the leading Pan-Africanists like Baraka argued for art that led to political liberation. (See, for example, Addison Gayle's *Black Aesthetic.*) Finally, Winston is fond of using Martin Luther King, Jr.'s last two years of life as a positive example of the success of black and white unity. There is no mention of King's opposition to Communism, his religious faith, his base in an all-black church or his bourgeois background.

9. See Chinua Achebe's novels, for example, *Things Fall Apart, No Longer at Ease.*

References

Abrahams, Roger D., ed. 1970. *Deep Down in the Jungle.* Chicago: Aldine.

Abramson, Paul. 1977. *The Political Socialization of Black Americans.* New York: MacMillan.

Adams, E. C. L. 1927. *Congaree Sketches.* Chapel Hill: University of North Carolina Press.

—. 1928. *Nigger to Nigger.* New York: Charles Scribner's Sons.

Agranoff, Robert, ed. 1972. *The New Style in Election Campaigns.* Boston: Holbrook.

Albritton, Robert B. 1979. "Social Amelioration through Mass Insurgency: A Re-examination of the Piven and Cloward Thesis." *American Political Science Review* 73, 1003-11.

Allen, Robert L. 1972. *Black Awakening in Capitalist America.* New York: Monthly Review Press.

Alleyne, Mervyn C. 1980. *Comparative Afro-American.* Ann Arbor: Karoma.

Amoda, Moyibi. 1972. *Black Politics and Black Vision.* Philadelphia: Westminster.

Anderson, Charles W. 1979. "The Place of Principles in Policy Analysis." *American Political Review* 73, 711-23.

Apostle, Richard A., et al. 1983. *The Anatomy of Racial Attitudes.* Berkeley: University of California Press.

Apter, David E., ed. 1964. *Ideology and Discontent.* New York: The Free Press.

Aptheker, Herbert., ed. 1968. *Marxism and Christianity.* New York: Humanities Press.

—. 1973. *Afro-American History.* Secaucus, New Jersey: Citadel.

Arendt, Hannah. 1963. *On Revolution.* New York: Viking.

Asante, Molefi Kete. 1980. *Afrocentricity.* Buffalo: Amulefi.

Babcock, Charles R. 1982. "The Melting Pot University." *This World,* 10 January.

Bacciocco, Edward J. 1974. *The New Left in America.* Stanford, California: Hoover Institute.

Bailey, Harry A., ed. 1967. *Negro Politics in America.* Columbus, Ohio: Merrill.

Bailey, Nan, et al. 1981. *The National Black Independent Political Party.* New York: Pathfinder.

Baker, Houston A., Jr. 1984. *Blues, Ideology and Afro-American Literature.* Chicago: University of Chicago Press.

Banfield, Edward. 1974. *The Unheavenly City.* Boston: Little, Brown.

—, and James Q. Wilson. 1963. *City Politics.* New York: Vintage.

Baraka, Amiri. 1974. "Revolutionary Culture and Future of Pan Afrikan Culture." Presented at the Sixth Pan-African Congress, Dar es Salaam, Tanzania, 19-27 June.

Baran, Paul, and Paul Sweezy. 1966. *Monopoly Capital.* New York: Monthly Review Press.

Barger, Harold M. 1974. "Images of the President and Policeman among Black, Mexican-American and Anglo School Children." Chicago: American Political Science Association Annual Meeting.

Barrera, Mario. 1979. *Race and Class in the Southwest.* Notre Dame: University of Notre Dame Press.

Bartley, Numan V., and Hugh D. Graham. 1975. *Southern Politics and the Second Reconstruction.* Baltimore: Johns Hopkins University.

Bayes, Jane H. 1982. *Minority Politics and Ideologies in the United States.* Novato, California: Chandler & Sharp.

Beauford, Fred. 1971. "An Interview With John A. Williams." *Black Creation* 2, no. 3 (Summer).

Bell, Daniel. 1965. *The End of Ideology.* New York: The Free Press.

——. 1975. "The Revolution of Rising Entitlements." *Fortune* 76 (April).

——. 1976. *The Cultural Contradiction of Capitalism.* New York: Basic Books.

Bellah, Robert N., et al. 1985. *Habits of the Heart.* New York: Harper & Row.

Benfell, Carol. 1984. "Reagan Sees Rights Laws Differently." *The Oakland Tribune,* 15 October.

Bennett, Lerone J. 1964. *What Manner of Man.* Chicago: Johnson Publishing Co.

Berelson, B. R., et al. 1954. *Voting.* Chicago: University of Chicago Press.

Bernstein, Richard J. 1975. "The Restructuring of Political Theory." Paper at the Annual Meeting of the American Political Science Association, San Francisco, September.

Berry, Mary Frances, and John W. Blassingame. 1982. *Long Memory.* New York: Oxford University Press.

Betts, Raymond F., ed. 1971. *The Ideology of Blackness.* Lexington, Massachusetts.: D. C. Heath.

Black Scholar. 1979. "The Black Sexism Debate." Vol. 10, nos. 8, 9.

Black, Albert, Jr. 1977. "Racism Has Not Declined, It Has Just Changed Its Form." *UMOJA* 1, no. 3.

Blair, Thomas L. 1977. *Retreat to the Ghetto.* New York: Hill and Wang.

Blalock, Hubert M. 1967. *Toward a Theory of Minority-Group Relations.* New York: Wiley & Sons.

Blassingame, John W. 1972. *The Slave Community.* New York: Oxford University Press.

Blauner, Robert. 1972. *Racial Oppression in America.* New York: Harper & Row.

Bluestein, Gene. 1972. *The Voice of Folk Art.* Amherst: University of Massachusetts Press.

Blumer, Herbert. 1958. "Racial Prejudice as a Sense of Group Position." *The Pacific Sociological Review* 1, no. 1.

Boggs, James. 1970. *Racism and the Class Struggle.* New York: Monthly Review Press.

Borders, William Holmes. 1944. *Seven Minutes at the 'Mike' in the Deep South.* Atlanta: Logan Press.

Boxill, Bernard R. 1984. *Blacks and Social Justice.* Totowa, New Jersey: Rowman & Allanheld.

Bozeman, Adda B. 1971. *The Future of Law in a Multicultural World.* Princeton: Princeton University Press.

——. 1976. *Conflict in Africa.* Princeton: Princeton University Press.

Bracey, John H., et al., eds. 1970. *Black Nationalism in America.* Indianapolis: Bobbs-Merrill.

Brawley, Edward M., ed. [1890] 1971. *The Negro Baptist Pulpit.* Freeport, New York: Books for Libraries Press.

Breitman, George. 1967. *The Last Year of Malcolm X.* New York: Merit.

——, ed. 1967. *Leon Trotsky on Black Nationalism and Self-Determination.* New York: Pathfinder.

Brigham, John, and Theodore Weisbach, eds. 1972. *Racial Attitudes in America.* New York: Harper & Row.

Brink, William, and Louis Harris. 1963. *The Negro Revolution in America.* New York: Simon and Schuster.

Broth, C. Anthony. 1987. *A Horse of a Different Color.* Washington, D.C.: Joint Center for Political Studies.

Brown, Egbert Ethelred. 1875-1956. Personal Papers, Schomburg Collection, New York Public Library.

Buckley, William F., Jr. 1968 edition. *Up From Liberalism.* New Rochelle, New York: Arlington House.

——, ed. 1970. *Did You Ever See a Dream Walking?* Indianapolis: Bobbs-Merrill.

Bullock, Charles S., and Harrell R. Rogers, Jr., eds. 1972. *Black Political Attitudes*. Chicago: Markham.

Bullock, Paul. 1966. *Watts: The Aftermath*. New York: Grove.

Bunche, Ralph J. 1928. "Negro Political Philosophy." Los Angeles: U.C.L.A. Archives, unpublished speech, Box 43.

——. 1929. "Marxism and the 'Negro Question.'" Unpublished paper, Ralph Bunche Collection, U.C.L.A., Box 133, Folder 4.

——. 1934. "The Philosophy of the New Deal." Unpublished speech, Ralph Bunche Collection, U.C.L.A.

——. 1935. "A Critical Analysis of the Tactics and Programs of Minority Groups." *The Journal of Negro Education* 4, no. 3, 308-20.

——. 1940. "The Framework for a Course on Negro History." Unpublished speech, Ralph Bunche Collection, U.C.L.A., Box 43.

——. 1941. "An Analysis of Contemporary Negro Leadership." Unpublished speech, Ralph Bunche Collection, U.C.L.A., Box 43.

Burgess, John M. 1982. *Black Gospel/White Church*. New York: Seabury.

Burgess, M. Elaine. 1962. *Negro Leadership in a Southern City*. Chapel Hill, North Carolina: University of North Carolina Press.

Burhman, Walter Dean. 1970. *Critical Elections and the Mainsprings of American Politics*. New York: Norton.

Burkett, Randall K. 1978. *Garveyism as a Religious Movement*. Metuchen, New Jersey: Scarecrow.

Burns, James MacGregor. 1978. *Leadership*. New York: Harper & Row.

Burton, Richard F. 1865. *Wit and Wisdom from West Africa*. London: Tinsley Bros.

Butterfield, Stephen. 1974. *Black Autobiography in America*. Amherst: University of Massachusetts Press.

CAAS Profile. 1984. "The 1984 National Black Election Study." Center for Afro-American and African Studies, University of Michigan, Fall.

Cabral, Amilcar. 1973. *Return to the Source*. New York: Monthly Review Press.

Campbell, Angus. 1971. *White Attitudes toward Black People*. Ann Arbor: IRS, University of Michigan.

Carlisle, Rodney. 1975. *The Roots of Black Nationalism*. Port Washington, New York: Kennikat.

Carmichael, Stokely, and Charles V. Hamilton. 1967. *Black Power*. New York: Vintage.

Carson, Clayborne. 1981. *In Struggle: SNCC and the Black Awakening of the 1960s*. Cambridge: Harvard University Press.

Cavanagh, Thomas. 1985. *Inside Black America*. Washington D.C.: Joint Center for Political Studies.

Cavanagh, Thomas E., and Lorn S. Foster. 1984. *Jesse Jackson's Campaign: The Primaries and Caucuses*. Washington, D.C.: Joint Center for Political Studies.

Chambers, William Nisbet, and Walter Dean Burnham, eds. 1975. *The American Party Systems*. New York: Oxford University Press.

Charters, Samuel. 1975. *The Legacy of the Blues*. London: Calder & Boyars.

Chernoff, John Miller. 1979. *African Rhythm and African Sensibility*. Chicago: University of Chicago Press.

Childs, John Brown. 1980. *The Political Black Minister*. Boston: G. K. Hall.

Chrisman, Robert, and Nathan Hare, eds. 1974. *Pan-Africanism*. Indianapolis: Bobbs-Merrill.

Civil Rights Documentation Project. 1967. "Interview with Ed Brown," Howard University, 20 June.

——. 1968. "Interview with Ella Baker," Howard University, 19 June.

Clark, Kenneth B. 1965. *Dark Ghetto: Dilemmas of Social Power*. New York: Harper.

——. 1974. *Pathos of Power*. New York: Harper.

——, and Jeanette Hopkins. 1968. *A Relevant War against Poverty*. New York: MARC & Harper.

Clarke, John Hendrick, ed. 1968. *William Styron's Turner*. Boston: Beacon.

Cleage, Albert B., Jr. 1968. *The Black Messiah*. New York: Sheed and Ward.

——. 1972. *Black Christian Nationalism*. New York: Morrow.

Cleaver, Elridge. 1968. *Soul on Ice*. New York: McGraw-Hill.

——. 1978. *Soul on Fire*. Waco, Texas: Word.

Cohen, Jerry, and William S. Murphy. 1966. *Burn, Baby, Burn!* New York: Dutton.

Cone, James H. 1969. *Black Theology & Black Power*. New York: Seabury.

——. 1972. *The Spirituals and the Blues*. New York: Seabury.

——. 1975. *God of the Oppressed*. London: Billing Sons.

——. 1982. *My Soul Looks Back*. Nashville: Abingdon.

Congress of African People. n.d. "Amiri Baraka Resigns as Secretary General of the National Black Assembly."

Conot, Robert. 1976. *Rivers of Blood Years of Darkness*. New York: Bantam.

Coser, Lewis A., and Irving Howe, eds. 1973. *The New Conservatives*. New York: Quadrangle/New York Times.

Courlander, Harold. 1963. *Negro Folk Music, U.S.A.* New York: Columbia University Press.

——. 1976. *A Treasury of Afro-American Folklore*. New York: Crown.

Cox, Oliver. [1948] 1970. *Caste, Class and Race*. New York: Modern Reader.

Cox, Richard H., ed. 1969. *Ideology, Politics, and Political Theory*. Belmont, California: Wadsworth.

Cronon, Edmund David. 1962. *Black Moses*. Madison: University of Wisconsin Press.

Crummey, Donald, ed. 1986. *Banditry, Rebellion and Social Protest in Africa*. London: James Currey.

Cruse, Harold. 1962. "Revolutionary Nationalism and the Afro- American." *Studies on the Left* 2, no. 3.

——. 1967. *The Crisis of the Negro Intellectual*. New York: Morrow.

——. 1969. *Rebellion or Revolution*. New York: Morrow.

——. 1971. "Black and White." *Black World* 20, no. 3 (January).

Dance, Daryl Cumber. 1978. *Shuckin' and Jivin'*. Bloomington: Indiana University Press.

——. 1987. *Long Gone*. Knoxville: University of Tennessee Press.

Daniels, Ron. n.d. "Revitalizing Independent Black Politics." National Black Political Assembly.

Davies, Alfred T., ed. 1965. *The Pulpit Speaks on Race*. New York: Abingdon Press.

Davis, Angela, ed. 1971. *If They Come in the Morning*. New York: Signet.

Davis, David B. 1966. *The Problem of Slavery in the Western Culture*. Ithaca, New York: Cornell University Press.

Davis, George, and Glegg Watson. 1982. *Black Life in Corporate America*. Garden City, New York: Doubleday.

Davis, Gerald L. 1985. *I Got the Word in Me and I Can Sing It, You Know*. Philadelphia: University of Pennsylvania Press.

Diamond, Martin. 1957. "A Response to McCloskey." *American Political Science Review* 50.

Dillard, J. L. 1977. *Lexicon of Black English*. New York: Seabury.

Dolbeare, Kenneth M., and Patricia Dolbeare. 1971. *American Ideologies*. Chicago: Markham.

Douglass, Frederick. 1968 *Narrative of the Life of Frederick Douglass*. New York: Signet.

Drake, St. Clair. 1970. *The Redemption of Africa and Black Religion.* Chicago: Third World.

Draper, Theodore. 1970. *The Rediscovery of Black Nationalism.* New York: Viking.

DuBois, W. E. B. 1898. *The Suppression of the African Slave-Trade.* Cambridge, Massachusetts: Harvard University Press.

Duff, John B., and Peter M. Mitchell, eds. 1971. *The Nat Turner Rebellion.* New York: Harper & Row.

Duncan, Hugh Dalziel. 1968. *Symbols in Society.* New York: Oxford University Press.

Dundes, Alan, ed. 1973. *Mother Wit from the Laughing Barrel.* Englewood Cliffs, New Jersey: Prentice-Hall.

Early, James. 1984. "Rainbow Politics: From Civil Rights to Civic Equality—An Interview with Jack O'Dell." *The Black Scholar* 15, no. 5 (September-October).

Easton, David. 1965a. *A Framework for Political Analysis.* Englewood Cliffs, New Jersey: Prentice-Hall.

—. 1965b. *A Systems Analysis of Political Life.* New York: Wiley & Sons.

Edelman, Murray. 1977. *Political Language.* New York: Academic Press.

Eisenstein, Aillah R., ed. 1978. "The Combahee River Collective." In *Capitalist Patriarchy and the Case of Socialist Feminism.* New York: Monthly Review Press.

Elder, John Dixon. 1968. "Martin Luther King and American Civil Religion." *Harvard Divinity School Bulletin* 1 (Spring), 17ff.

Ellison, Ralph. 1952. *Invisible Man.* New York: Signet.

—. 1966 edition. *Shadow and Act.* New York: Signet.

Epstein, Dena J. 1977. *Sinful Tunes and Spirituals.* Urbana, Illinois: University of Illinois Press.

Essien-Udom, E. U. 1962. *Black Nationalism.* New York: Dell.

Evans, Sarah. 1979. *Personal Politics.* New York: Knopf.

Fairmont Papers. 1980. *Black Alternatives Conference.* San Francisco Institute for Contemporary Studies, December.

Fanon, Frantz. 1967. *Black Skin, White Masks.* New York: Grove.

Farrar, Eleanor. 1971. "Report of the Washington Office of MARC Inc."

Feagin, Joe R., and Harlan Hahn. 1973. *Ghetto Revolts.* New York: MacMillan.

Feuer, Lewis S. 1975. *Ideology and Ideologists.* New York: Harper & Row.

FOCUS. 1984. "JCPS Survey of Political Attitudes." Joint Center for Political Studies, September.

Fogelson, Robert. 1969. *Mass Violence in America.* New York: Arno and New York Times.

Forman, James. 1972. *The Making of Black Revolutionaries.* New York: MacMillan.

Fortune, Timothy Thomas. [1884] 1968. *Black and White.* New York: Arno and New York Times.

Franklin, H. Bruce. 1978. *The Victim as Criminal and Artists.* New York: Oxford University Press.

Franklin, Raymond S., and Solomon Resnik. 1973. *The Political Economy of Racism.* New York: Holt, Rinehart and Winston.

Franklin, V. P. 1984. *Black Self-Determination.* Westport, Connecticut: Lawrence Hill.

Frazier, E. Franklin. 1939. *The Negro Family in the United States.* Chicago: University of Chicago Press.

—. 1963. *The Negro Church in America.* New York: Schocken.

Fredrickson, George M. 1971. *The Black Image in the White Mind.* New York: Harper & Row.

Freeman, Jo. n.d. "The Political Culture of the Democratic and Republican Parties." Unpublished manuscript.

—. 1975. *The Politics of Women's Liberation.* New York: McKay.

Freire, Paulo. 1968. *Pedagogy of the Oppressed.* New York: Seabury.

Gandhi, Mohandas K. 1957. *An Autobiography: The Story of My Experiments with Truth.* Boston: Beacon.

Gans, Herbert J. 1974. *Popular Culture and High Culture.* New York: Basic Books.

Garon, Paul. 1979. *Blues & the Poetic Spirit.* New York: DaCapo.

Garrow, David J. 1978. *Protest at Selma: Martin Luther King, Jr., and the Voting Rights Act of 1965.* New Haven: Yale University Press.

——. 1981. *The FBI and Martin Luther King, Jr.* New York: Penguin.

Garvey, Marcus. 1968. *Philosophy and Opinions of Marcus Garvey.* New York: Arno and New York Times.

Geertz, Clifford, ed. 1963. *Old Societies and New States.* New York: The Free Press of Glencoe.

——. 1973. *The Interpretation of Cultures.* New York: Basic.

Geiss, Imanuel. 1974. *The Pan-African Movement.* New York: Africana.

Gendzier, Irene. 1973. *Frantz Fanon: A Critical Study.* New York: Pantheon.

Genovese, Eugene D. 1976. *Roll, Jordan, Roll.* New York: Vintage.

George, Herman, Jr. 1984. *American Race Relations Theory: A Review of Four Models.* Westport, Connecticut: Greenwood.

Gilliam, Reginald E., Jr. 1975. *Black Political Development.* Port Washington, New York: Kennikat.

Gilmore, Al Tony. 1975. *Bad Nigger!: The National Impact of Jack Johnson.* Port Washington, New York: Kennikat.

Githens, Marianne. 1982. "Politics and Gender." Paper presented at the Annual Meeting of the American Political Science Association, Denver, 2-5 September.

Glasgow, Douglas G. 1981. *The Black Underclass.* New York: Vintage.

Glazer, Nathan, and Daniel P. Moynihan. 1963. *Beyond the Melting Pot.* Cambridge, Massachusetts: MIT and Harvard University.

Goldfarb, Jeffrey C. 1982. *On Cultural Freedom.* Chicago: University of Chicago Press.

Goldman, Peter. 1979. *The Death and Life of Malcolm X.* Urbana: University of Illinois.

Goldstein, Michael. 1981. "The Political Careers of Fred Roberts and Tom Bradley." *The Western Journal of Black Studies* 5, no. 2 (Summer), 139-46.

Goldstein, Rhoda L., ed. 1971. *Black Life and Culture in the United States.* New York: Crowell.

Gordon, Vivan Verdell, ed. 1979. *Lectures: Black Scholars on Black Issues.* Washington, D.C.: University Press of America.

Gosnell, Harold F. [1935] 1967. *Negro Politicians.* Chicago: University of Chicago Press.

Gould, James A., and Willis H. Truitt, eds. 1973. *Political Ideologies.* New York: MacMillan.

Gouldner, Alvin W. 1970. *The Coming Crisis of Western Sociology.* New York: Avon.

——. 1976. *The Dialectic of Ideology and Technology.* New York: Seabury.

Gramsci, Antonio. 1971. *Selections from the Prison Notebooks.* Edited and translated by Quentin Hoare and Geoffrey Nowell Smith. New York: International Publications.

Greenberg, Edward S. 1970. "Orientations of Black and White Children to Political Authority Figures." *Social Science Quarterly* 51.

Greenstone, J. David, and Paul E. Peterson. 1973. *Race and Authority in Urban Politics.* New York: Sage.

Gross, Bertram. 1980. *Friendly Fascism.* Boston: South End.

Gross, Jonathan L., and Steve Rayner. 1985. *Measuring Culture.* New York: Columbia University Press.

Gutman, Herbert G. 1976. *The Black Family in Slavery and Freedom, 1750-1925.* New York: Pantheon.

Gwaltney, John Langston. 1981. *Drylongso.* New York: Vintage.

Halisi, Clyde, and James Mtume, eds. 1967. *The Quotable Karenga.* Los Angeles: US.

Hall, Raymond L., ed. 1974. *Black Separatism and Social Reality.* New York: Pergamon.

Hamilton, Charles V. 1972. *The Black Preacher in America.* New York: Morrow.

—. 1982. "Measuring Black Conservatism." *The State of Black America 1982.* New York: National Urban League.

Hannerz, Ulf. 1969. *Soulside.* New York: Columbia University Press.

Hanson, Eric. 1988. "James Baldwin and the Blues." *The Williams Journal of Afro-American Studies* 1, no. 1 (Spring).

Haralambos, Michael. 1974. *Right On: From Blues to Soul in Black America.* London: Eddison.

Harding, Vincent. 1981. *There Is a River.* New York: Vintage.

Harlan, Louis R. 1972. *Booker T. Washington.* New York: Oxford University Press.

Harris, Leonard, ed. 1983. *Philosophy Born of Struggle.* Dubuque, Iowa: Kendall/Hunt.

Harris, Marvin. 1980. *Cultural Materialism.* New York: Vintage.

Harris, Norman. 1974. "A Recurring Malady: Baraka's Move to the Left." *Endarch* 1, no. 1 (Fall).

Hart, Roderick P. 1977. *The Political Pulpit.* West Lafayette, Indiana: Purdue University Press.

Hartz, Louis. 1955. *The Liberal Tradition in America.* New York: Harcourt, Brace & World.

Henderson, Stephen. 1973. *Understanding the New Black Poetry.* New York: Morrow.

Henry, Charles P. 1974. "An Event-Oriented Approach to Black Politics." Unpublished Ph.D. diss., University of Chicago.

—. 1979. "Big Philanthropy and the Funding of Black Organizations." *The Review of Black Political Economy* 9, no. 2 (Winter), 174-90.

—. 1981. "Ebony Elite: America's Most Influential Blacks." *Phylon* 42, no. 2 (Summer), 120-32.

—. 1983. "Racial Factors in the 1982 California Gubernatorial Campaign." Paper presented at the Western Political Science Association annual meeting, Seattle, Washington.

Henry, Jules. 1963. *Culture against Man.* New York: Vintage.

Herskovits, Melville J. 1958. *The Myth of the Negro Past.* Boston: Beacon.

Herzog, George. 1936. *Jabo Proverbs from Liberia.* London: Oxford University Press.

Hill, Robert A. 1983. *The Marcus Garvey and Universal Negro Improvement Association Papers,* vol. 1. Berkeley: University of California Press.

Hobsbawn, E. J. 1959. *Primitive Rebels.* New York: Norton.

Holden, Matthew, Jr. 1973. *The Politics of the Black "Nation."* New York: Chandler.

Holt, Len. 1965. *The Summer that Didn't End.* New York: Morrow.

Holt, Thomas. 1977. *Black over White.* Urbana: University of Illinois Press.

Hooks, Bell. 1981. *Ain't I a Woman.* Boston: South End.

Hughes, Langston, ed. 1961. *An African Treasury.* New York: Pyramid.

Hughes, Langston, and Arna Bontemps, eds. 1958. *The Book of Negro Folklore.* New York: Dodd, Mead.

Huntington, Samuel P. 1975. "The Democratic Distemper." *The Public Interest* 41 (Fall).

Hurston, Zora Neale. 1965. *Their Eyes Were Watching God.* Greenwich, Connecticut: Fawcett.

Hyman, Stanley Edgar. 1978. *The Critics Credentials.* New York: Atheneum.

Jackson, Bruce. 1974a. *Get Your Ass in the Water and Swim Like Me.* Cambridge, Massachusetts: Harvard University Press.

—, ed. 1974b. *Wake Up Dead Man.* Cambridge, Massachusetts: Harvard University Press.

Jackson, George. 1970. *Soledad Brother.* New York: Coward-McCann.

Jackson '84. n.d. "A Preliminary Review." Washington, D.C.: Jesse Jackson for President Committee.

Jackson, M. Njeri. 1982. "Black Feminist Ideology." Paper presented at the Annual Meeting of the National Conference of Black Political Scientists, New Orleans, 23 April.

Jahn, Janheinz. 1961. *MUNTU* New York: Grove.

Johnson, Guy B. 1937. "Negro Racial Movements and Leadership in the United States." *American Journal of Sociology* 43, 57-71.

Johnson, Haynes, and Thomas B. Edsall. 1984. "North Carolina Contests Sparks Registration War." *Washington Post*, 30 September.

Johnson, John Albert. 1857-1928. Personal Papers, Schomburg Collection, New York Public Library.

Joint Center for Political Studies. 1984. "JCPS Survey of Political Attitudes." *Focus*, September.

Jones, LeRoi. 1963. *Blues People.* New York: Morrow.

—. 1966. *Home.* New York: Morrow.

Jones, LeRoi, and Larry Neal, eds. 1968. *Black Fire.* New York: Morrow.

Jones, Rhett S. 1988. "In the Absence of Ideology." *The Western Journal of Black Studies* 12, no. 1.

Jordan, Wintrop. 1968. *White over Black.* Baltimore: Pelican.

July, Robert W. 1967. *The Origins of Modern African Thought.* New York: Praeger.

—. 1987. *An African Voice.* Durham: Duke University Press.

Karenga, M. Ron. 1977. "Afro-American Nationalism." *Black Books Bulletin* 6, no. 1 (Spring).

—. 1978. *Essays on Struggle.* San Diego: Kawaida.

—. 1979. "The Socio-Political Philosophy of Malcolm X." *The Western Journal of Black Studies* 3, no. 4 (Winter).

—. 1984. "Jesse Jackson and the Presidential Campaign." *The Black Scholar* 15, no. 5 (September-October).

Katznelson, Ira. 1981. *City Trenches.* Chicago: University of Chicago Press.

Keil, Charles. 1966. *Urban Blues.* Chicago: University of Chicago Press.

Kent, George. 1972. *Blackness and the Adventure of Western Culture.* Chicago: Third World Press.

King, Coretta Scott. 1969. *My Life with Martin Luther King, Jr.* New York: Holt, Rinehart & Winston.

King, Martin Luther, Jr. 1958. *Stride toward Freedom: The Montgomery Story.* New York: Harper & Row.

—. 1959. *The Measure of Man.* Philadelphia: Christian Education Press.

—. 1963a. *Strength to Love.* New York: Harper & Row.

—. 1963b. *Why We Can't Wait.* New York: Harper & Row.

—. 1967a. *The Trumpet of Conscience.* New York: Harper & Row.

—. 1967b. *Where Do We Go from Here: Chaos or Community.* New York: Harper & Row.

King, Martin Luther, Sr. 1980. *Daddy King: An Autobiography.* New York: Morrow.

Kirk, Russell. 1974. *The Roots of American Order.* La Salle, Illinois: Open Court.

Kluger, Richard. 1976. *Simple Justice.* New York: Knopf.

Kochman, Thomas. 1981. *Black and White Styles in Conflict.* Chicago: University of Chicago Press.

Kofsky, Frank. 1970. *Black Nationalism and the Revolution in Music.* New York: Pathfinder Press.

Kopkind, Andrew, and Alexander Cockburn. 1984. "The Left, the Democrats & the Future." *The Nation,* 21-28 July.

Kornhauser, William. 1959. *The Politics of Mass Society.* Glencoe, Illinois: The Free Press.

Kusmer, Kenneth L. 1976. *A Ghetto Takes Shape.* Urbana, Illinois: University of Illinois Press.

Labov, William. 1972. "Rules for Ritual Insults." In Thomas Kochman, ed., *Rappin' and Stylin' Out.* Urbana, Illinois: University of Illinois Press, 265-314.

Ladd, Everett Carll, Jr. 1966. *Negro Political Leadership in the South.* Ithaca, New York: Cornell University Press.

Ladd, Everett Carll, Jr., with Charles D. Hadley. 1978. *Transformation of the American Party Systems.* New York: Norton.

Ladner, Joyce, ed. 1973. *The Death of White Sociology.* New York: Vintage.

Lattin, Don. 1988. "Mythologist's Sudden New Appeal." *San Francisco Chronicle,* 15 August, A4.

Leab, Daniel J. 1976. *From Sambo to Superspade.* Boston: Houghton Mifflin.

Leacock, Elenor Burke, ed. 1971. *The Culture of Poverty: A Critique.* New York: Simon and Schuster.

Leslau, Charlotte, and Wolf Leslau, eds. 1962. *African Proverbs.* Mount Vernon, New York: Peter Pauper.

Levine, Charles H. 1974. *Racial Conflict and the American Mayor.* Lexington, Massachusetts: D. C. Heath.

Levine, Lawrence W. 1977. *Black Culture and Black Consciousness.* New York: Oxford University Press.

Levintan, Sar A., and Robert Taggart. 1976. *The Promise of Greatness.* Cambridge, Massachusetts: Harvard University Press.

Levy, Mark R., and Michael S. Kramer. 1973. *The Ethnic Factor.* New York: Simon and Schuster.

Lewis, David L. 1970. *King: A Critical Biography.* Baltimore: Penguin.

Lewy, Guenter. 1974. *Religion and Revolution.* New York: Oxford University Press.

Liebow, Elliot. 1967. *Tally's Corner.* Boston: Little, Brown.

Lincoln, C. Eric. 1973. *The Black Muslims in America.* Boston: Beacon.

—, ed. 1974. *The Black Experience in Religion.* Garden City, New Jersey: Anchor.

Lindblom, Charles E., and David K. Cohen. 1979. *Usable Knowledge.* New Haven: Yale University Press.

Line of March. 1984. "The New Motion in Black Politics and the Electoral Arena." No. 15 (Spring).

Lipsky, Michael. 1968. "Protest as a Political Resource." *American Political Science Review* 62 (December), 1051-61.

Locke, Alain. [1925] 1968. *The New Negro.* New York: Atheneum.

Lomax, Louis. 1962. *The Negro Revolt.* New York: Signet.

Long, Charles H. 1971. "Perspectives for a Study of Afro-American Religion in the United States." *History of Religions* 11, no. 1 (August).

Long, Richard A. n.d. "The Symbolization of Black Consciousness." UCAAS Occasional Paper no. 12.

Loury, Glenn C. 1985. "The Moral Quandary of the Black Community." *Public Interest* (Spring).

Lovell, John, Jr. 1972. *Black Song.* New York: MacMillan.

Lowi, Theodore J. 1964. "American Business, Public Policy, Case-Studies, and Political Theory." *World Politics* 16, no. 4 (July).

—. 1984. "Why Is There No Socialism in the United States? A Federal Analysis." *International Political Science Review* 5, no. 4.

Lyman, Stanford M. 1972. *The Black American in Sociological Thought.* New York: Putnam's Sons.

MacRae, Duncan. 1976. *The Social Function of Social Science.* New Haven: Yale University Press.

Malcolm X, with the assistance of Alex Haley. 1965. *The Autobiography of Malcolm X.* New York: Grove.

Mannheim, Karl. 1936. *Ideology and Utopia.* New York: Harcourt, Brace & World.

Marable, Manning. 1980. "Beyond Coalition: Toward a New Strategy for Black Nationalist Politics." *First World* 2, no. 4 (January).

———. 1983. *How Capitalism Underdeveloped Black America.* Boston: South End.

———. 1985. *Black American Politics.* London: Verso.

Marcuse, Herbert. 1974. *One-Dimensional Man.* Boston: Beacon.

Marine, Gene. 1969. *The Black Panthers.* New York: New American Library.

Martin, Tony. 1976. *Race First.* Westport, Connecticut: Greenwood.

Matthews, William. 1984. "Glenn: Democrats Must Change." *The Sunday Advocate,* 11 November.

Mays, Benjamin E. 1968. *The Negro's God.* New York: Atheneum.

Mazmanian, Daniel A. 1974. *Third Parties in Presidential Elections.* Washington, D.C.: Brookings.

Mazrui, Ali A. 1974. *World Culture and the Black Experience.* Seattle: University of Washington.

McAdam, Doug. 1982. *Political Process and the Development of Black Insurgency, 1930-1970.* Chicago: University of Chicago Press.

McClosky, Herbert. 1957. "American Political Thought and the Study of Politics." *American Political Science Review* 50.

McMurry, Linda O. 1981. *George Washington Carver.* New York: Oxford University Press.

McWilliams, Wilson Carey. 1973. *The Idea of Fraternity in America.* Berkeley: University of California Press.

Meier, August. 1965. "On the Role of Martin Luther King." *New Politics* 4 (Winter), 52ff.

Meier, August, and Elliott Rudwick. 1973. *C.O.R.E.* New York: Oxford University Press.

Memmi, Albert. 1965. *The Colonizer and the Colonized.* New York: Orion Press.

Merelman, Richard M. 1984. *Making Something of Ourselves.* Berkeley: University of California Press.

Miller, Kelley. [1908] 1968. *Radicals and Conservatives and Other Essays on the Negro in America.* New York: Schocken.

———. 1971 edition. *Out of the House of Bondage.* New York: Schocken.

Miller, William Robert. 1968. *Martin Luther King, Jr.: His Life Martyrdom and Meaning for the World.* New York: Weybright and Talley.

Mitchell, Henry H. 1970. *Black Preaching.* Philadelphia: Lippincott.

———. 1975. *Black Belief.* New York: Harper & Row.

Morris, Lorenzo. 1974. "The Invisible Politics: Culture and Political Participation in Black and White America." Revised Ph.D. diss., University of Chicago.

———. 1977. "Culture and Ideology in Marx's Social Science." Presented at the Annual Meeting of the National Conference of Black Political Scientists in Atlanta, Georgia, March.

———. 1984. "The Emergence of Ideology in Presidential Politics." *Urban League Review* 8, no. 3 (Summer).

———, and Charles Henry. 1978. *The Chit'lin Controversy: Race and Public Policy in America.* Washington, D.C.: University Press of America.

Morris, Milton D. 1975. *The Politics of Black America.* New York: Harper & Row.

Moses, Wilson Jeremiah. 1978. *The Golden Age of Black Nationalism 1850-1925.* Hamden, Connecticut: Anchon.

———. 1982. *Black Messiahs and Uncle Toms.* University Park, Pennsylvania: Pennsylvania State University Press.

Mouffe, Chabtal, ed. 1979. *Gramsci and Marxist Theory.* London: Routledge & Kegan Paul.

Moynihan, Daniel P. 1969. *Maximum Feasible Misunderstanding.* New York: The Free Press.

Mueller, Claus. 1973. *The Politics of Communication.* New York: Oxford University Press.

Murray, Albert. 1971. *The Omni-Americans.* New York: Avon.

———. 1973. *The Hero and the Blues.* University of Missouri Press.

———. 1976. *Stomping the Blues.* New York: McGraw-Hill.

Murray, Charles. 1984. *Losing Ground.* New York: Basic Books.

Myrdal, Gunnar. 1964. *An American Dilemma.* New York: Harper & Row.

National Black Political Assembly. n.d. "New Politics for Black People."

Nellis, John R. 1972. *A Theory of Ideology.* Nairobi: Oxford University Press.

Nelson, Jack. 1982. "Democratic Pollster: Blacks Hate Reagan." [Berkeley] *Daily Californian,* 5 October.

Nelson, Hart M., et al., eds. 1971. *The Black Church in America.* New York: Basic Books.

Nelson, Hart M., and Anne Kusener Nelson. 1975. *The Black Church in the Sixties.* Lexington, Kentucky: University Press of Kentucky.

Nelson, Richard R. 1977. *The Moon and the Ghetto.* New York: Norton.

Nelson, William Stuart. 1970. "Martin Luther King." *Political Science Review* 9 (January-June), 166-72.

Newbold, Robert T., Jr., ed. 1977. *Black Preaching.* Philadelphia: Geneva Press.

Newfield, Jack. 1966. *A Prophetic Minority.* New York: Signet.

Newsweek. 1981. "The Black Conservatives," 9 March.

Nichol, John Thomas. 1966. *Pentecostalism.* New York: Harper & Row.

Nisbet, Robert. 1976. *Sociology as an Art Form.* New York: Oxford University Press.

Nketia, J. H. Kwabena. 1974. *The Music of Africa.* New York: Norton.

Nyerere, Julius. 1974. "Speech to the Pan-African Congress." Ministry of Information and Broadcasting, Dar es Salaam, Tanzania, 19 June.

Oates, Stephen B. 1982. *Let the Trumpet Sound: The Life of Martin Luther King, Jr.* New York: Harper & Row.

Oakley, Giles. 1977. *The Devil's Music.* New York: Taplinger.

Oliver, Paul. 1960. *The Meaning of the Blues.* New York: Collier.

Olson, Marcus. 1973. *The Logic of Collective Action.* Cambridge, Massachusetts: Harvard University Press.

Orbell, John. 1967. "Protest Participation among Southern Negro College Students." *American Political Science Review* 61.

Padmore, George. 1972. *Pan-Africanism or Communism.* Garden City, New York: Anchor.

Paris, Peter J. 1985. *The Social Teaching of the Black Churches.* Philadelphia: Fortress Press.

Parsons, Talcott. 1959. "An Approach to the Sociology of Knowledge." *Transactions of the Fourth World Congress of Sociology,* Milan.

Patterson, Orlando. 1973. "The Moral Crisis of the Black American." *Public Interest* 32.

Pease, Jane H., and William H. Pease. 1974. *They Who Would Be Free.* New York: Atheneum.

Perlo, Victor. 1975. *Economics of Racism.* New York: International Publishers.

Perry, James. 1982. "Bradley's Quiet Style Reassures Many Voters in California Campaign." *Wall Street Journal,* 11 October.

Peterson, Paul E. 1979. "Organizational Imperatives and Ideological Change." *Urban Affairs Quarterly* 14, no. 4 (June).

Philips, Kevin. 1969. *The Emergent Republican Majority.* New York: Arlington.

Pinkney, Alphonso. 1976. *Red, Black and Green.* New York: Cambridge University Press.

Piven, Francis Fox, and Richard A. Cloward. 1971. *Regulating the Poor: The Functions of Public Welfare.* New York: Pantheon.

——. 1979. *Poor People's Movements.* New York: Vintage.

——. 1982. *The New Class War.* New York: Pantheon.

Polsby, Nelson W., and Aaron Wildavsky. 1976. *Presidential Elections.* New York: Scribner's.

Porter, Thomas. 1977. "The Social Roots of Afro-American Music: 1950-1970." In Ernest Kaiser, ed., *A Freedomways Reader.* New York: International.

Preston, Michael B., et al., eds. 1982. *The New Black Politics.* New York: Longman.

Puckett, Newbell Niles. 1926. *Folk Beliefs of the Southern Negro.* Chapel Hill: University of North Carolina Press.

Quarles, Benjamin. 1969. *Black Abolitionists.* New York: Oxford University Press.

Quinones, Miriam Louis, et al. 1984. "Women's Stake in the Rainbow." *The Black Scholar* 15, no. 5, September-October.

Raboteau, Albert J. 1978. *Slave Religion.* New York: Oxford University Press.

Raines, Howell, ed. 1977. *My Soul Is Rested.* New York: Bantam.

Rainwater, Lee, and William L. Yancey. 1966. "Black Families and the White House." *TRANS-action* 3, no. 5.

——. 1967. *The Moynihan Report and the Politics of Controversy.* Cambridge, Massachusetts: MIT Press.

Redmond, Eugene B. 1976. *Drumvoices.* New York: Anchor.

Reed, Aldolph, Jr. 1986. *The Jesse Jackson Phenomenon.* New Haven: Yale University Press.

Rein, Martin. 1976. *Social Science and Public Policy.* New York: Penguin.

Reynolds, Barbara. 1975. *Jesse Jackson: The Man, the Movement, the Myth.* Chicago: Nelson-Hall.

Roberts, John Storm. 1972. *Black Music of Two Worlds.* New York: Praeger.

Roberts, John W. 1982. "Black Folklore and Song." *The Western Journal of Black Studies* 6, no. 2, 101-107.

Robinson, Cedric J. 1983. *Black Marxism.* London: ZED.

Rodman, Hyman. 1963. "The Lower-Class Value Stretch." *Social Forces,* December, 205-15.

Rogin, Michael Paul. 1967. *The Intellectuals and McCarthy.* Clinton, Massachusetts: MIT Press.

Rosenbaum, Walter A. 1975. *Political Culture.* New York: Praeger.

Rossiter, Clinton. 1962. *Conservatism in America.* New York: Vintage.

Rude, George. 1980. *Ideology and Popular Protest.* New York: Pantheon.

Rubenstein, Richard. 1970. *Rebels in Eden.* Boston: Little, Brown.

Said, Edward W. 1979. *Orientalism.* New York: Vintage.

Sartre Jean-Paul. 1963. *Saint Genet.* New York: Braziller.

Scammon, Richard M., and Ben J. Wattenberg. 1971. *The Real Majority.* New York: Coward, McCann and Geoghegan.

Schneider, William. 1984a. "The Dividing Line between Delegates Is Age." *National Journal Convention Daily,* 16 July.

——. 1984b. "How Farrakhan Divides the Delegates." *National Journal Convention Daily,* 17 July.

Schuman, Howard, and Shirley Hatchett. 1974. *Black Racial Attitudes, Trends, and Complexities.* Ann Arbor: IRS, University of Michigan.

Schuman, Howard, et al. 1985. *Racial Attitudes in America.* Cambridge, Massachusetts: Harvard University Press.

Schuyler, George S. 1966. *Black and Conservative*. New Rochelle, New York: Arlington House.

Scott, Manuel L. 1973. *The Gospel for the Ghetto*. Nashville: Broadman.

Scott, Robert L., and Wayne Brockriede, eds. 1969. *The Rhetoric of Black Power*. New York: Harper & Row.

Seltzer, Richard, and Robert C. Smith. 1985. "Race and Ideology." *Phylon* 46, no. 2 (Summer).

Sernett, Milton C. 1975. *Black Religion and American Evangelicalism*. Metuchen, New Jersey: Scarecrow.

Sharma, Mohan L. 1968. "Martin Luther King: Modern America's Greatest Theologian of Social Action." *Journal of Negro History* 53, 255-63.

Shepperson, George. 1960. "Notes on Negro American Influence of African Nationalism." *Journal of African History* 1, no. 2, 299-312.

Sherman, Richard B. 1973. *The Republican Party and Black America*. Charlottesville: University Press of Virginia.

Sherwood, Tom. 1984. "Jackson Says He's Hindered by Stereotypes." *The Oakland Tribune*, 22 March.

Shils, Edward. 1958. "Ideology and the Intellectual." *Daedalus*.

Sibley, Mulford Q. 1970. "An Exegesis of Martin Luther King, Jr.'s Social Philosophy." *Phylon* 31 (January-June), 89ff.

Silberman, Charles E. 1980. *Criminal Violence, Criminal Justice*. New York: Vintage.

Singham, A. H. 1967. "The Political Socialization of Marginal Groups." *International Journal of Comparative Sociology* 8.

Skelton, Nancy. 1984. "Jackson Blames News Media for Outsider Status." *The Oakland Tribune*, 20 March.

Smelser, Neil. 1962. *A Theory of Collective Behavior*. New York: Free Press.

Smith, C. S., ed. 1888. *Bishop Daniel Payne Sermons Delivered before the General Conference of the A.M.E. Church*. Nashville, Tennessee: African Methodist Episcopal Church.

Smith, Earl. 1977. "Roll, Apology, Roll." In Ernest Kaiser, ed., *A Freedomways Reader*. New York: International.

Smith, Ervin. 1981. *The Ethics of Martin Luther King, Jr*. New York: Edwin Mellon.

Smith, J. Alfred, Sr., ed. 1976. *Outstanding Black Sermons*. Valley Forge: Judson.

Smith, Kenneth L., and Ira G. Zepp, Jr. 1974. *Search for the Beloved Community: The Thinking of Martin Luther King, Jr*. Valley Forge: Judson.

Smith, Timothy L. 1972. "Slavery and Theology." *Church History* 41, no. 4 (December).

———. 1978. "Religion and Ethnicity in America." *The American Historical Review* 83, no. 5 (December).

Sniderman, Paul M., with Michael Hagen. 1985. *Race and Inequality*. Chatham, New Jersey: Chatham House.

Sollars, Werner. 1986. *Beyond Ethnicity*. New York: Oxford University Press.

Southern, Eileen. 1971. *The Music of Black Americans*. New York: Norton.

Sowell, Thomas. 1972. *Black Education: Myths and Tragedies*. New York: McKay.

———. 1975. *Race and Economics*. New York: McKay.

Starling, Grover. 1979. *The Politics and Economics of Public Policy*. Homewood, Illinois: Dorsey.

Stein, Judith. 1986. *The World of Marcus Garvey*. Baton Rouge: Louisiana State University Press.

Steinfels, Peter. 1979. *The Neoconservatives*. New York: Simon and Schuster.

Stepto, Robert. 1979. *From Behind the Veil*. Urbana, Illinois: University of Illinois Press.

Stewart, James T. 1968. "The Development of the Black Revolutionary Artist." In LeRoi Jones and Larry Neal, eds., *Black Fire*. New York: Morrow.

Stewart, John G. 1974. *One Last Chance.* New York: Praeger.

Stoper, Emily. 1977. "The Student Nonviolent Coordinating Committee." *Journal of Black Studies* 8, no. 1.

Storing, Herbert J., ed. 1970. *What Country Have I?* New York: St. Martins.

Stuckey, Sterling. 1968. "Through the Prism of Folklore." *Massachusetts Review* 9.

——. 1969. *Proceedings of the Summer Institutes in Afro-American Studies, Brooklyn College,* 1.

——, ed. 1972. *The Ideological Origins of Black Nationalism.* Boston: Beacon.

——. 1987. *Slave Culture.* New York: Oxford University Press.

Styron, William. 1966. *The Confessions of Nat Turner.* New York: Signet.

Sundquist, James L. 1973. *Dynamics of the Party System.* Washington, D.C.: Brookings.

Sutton, F. X., et al. 1956. *The American Business Creed.* Cambridge, Massachusetts: Harvard University Press.

Sweet, Leonard I. 1976. *Black Images of America 1784-1870.* New York: W. W. Norton.

Synan, Vinson. 1971. *The Holiness-Pentecostal Movement.* Grand Rapids, Michigan: Eerdmans.

Szalay, Lorand B., et al. 1972. "Ideology: Its Meaning and Measurement." *Comparative Political Studies* (July).

——, and Bela C. Maday. 1983. "Implicit Culture and Psychocultural Distance." *American Anthropologist* 85, no. 1 (March).

Tabb, William K. 1970. *The Political Economy of the Black Ghetto.* New York: Norton.

Takula, H. S. 1970. "The Place of Martin Luther King in the Negroes' Struggle for Equality." *Political Science Review* 9 (January-June), 136-65.

Tarrance, V. Lance, and Walter de Vries. 1972. *The Split-Ticket Voter.* Grand Rapids, Michigan: Eerdmans.

Thompson, Daniel C. 1963. *The Negro Leadership Class.* Englewood Cliffs, New Jersey: Prentice-Hall.

Thompson, John B. 1984. *Studies in Theory of Ideology.* Berkeley: University of California Press.

Thompson, Robert Farris. 1984. *Flash of the Spirit.* New York: Vintage.

TIME. 1987. "Attitudes in Black and White," 2 February.

Tinney, James. 1977. "A Theoretical and Historical Comparison of Black Political and Religious Movements." Unpublished Ph.D. diss., Howard University.

Tocqueville, Alexis de. 1956, Heffner edition. *Democracy in America.* New York: Mentor.

Toll, William. 1979. *The Resurgence of Race.* Philadelphia: Temple University Press.

Toure, Sekou. 1974. "A Dialectical Approach to Culture." In Robert Chrisman and Nathan Hare, eds., *Pan-Africanism.* Indianapolis: Bobbs-Merrill.

Turner, James. 1971. "Black Nationalism." *Black World,* January.

Valentine, Charles A. 1968. *Culture and Poverty.* Chicago: University of Chicago Press.

Van de Berghe, Pierre L. 1967. *Race and Racism.* New York: Wiley & Sons.

Verba, Sidney, and Gary R. Orren. 1985. *Equality in America.* Cambridge: Harvard University Press.

Vincent, Theodore G. 1971. *Black Power and the Garvey Movement.* Berkeley: Ramparts.

Wagstaff, Thomas, ed. 1969. *Black Power.* Beverly Hills: Glencoe.

Walker, Clarence E. 1980. "Massa's New Clothes." *UMOJA* 4, no. 2 (Summer).

Walker, Eugene P. 1978. "A History of the Southern Christian Leadership Conference, 1955-1965." Unpublished Ph.D. diss., Duke University.

Walters, Ronald. 1984. "Strategy for 1976: A Black Political Party." *The Black Scholar* 15, no. 4 (July-August).

——. n.d. "Afro-American Nationalism." Washington D.C.: Howard University.

Walton, Hanes, Jr. 1972. *Black Politics.* Philadelphia: Lippincott.
——. 1985. *Invisible Politics.* Albany: State University of New York.
Washington, Booker T. 1899. *The Future of the American Negro.* Boston: Small, Maynard.
Washington, Joseph R., Jr. 1964. *Black Religion.* Boston: Beacon.
——. 1967. *The Politics of God.* Boston: Beacon.
Watters, Pat, and Reese Cleghorn. 1967. *Climbing Jacob's Ladder.* New York: Harcourt, Brace & World.
Weber, Max. 1958. *The Protestant Ethic and the Spirit of Capitalism.* New York: Charles Scribner's Sons.
Weiss, Nancy J. 1983. *Farewell to the Party of Lincoln.* Princeton: Princeton University Press.
Welch, Susan, and Michael W. Combs. 1985. "Intra-racial Differences in Attitudes of Blacks." *Phylon* 46, no. 2 (Summer).
White, Theodore Hill. 1984. "The Shaping of the Presidency 1984." *TIME,* 19 November.
Whitting, C. E. J. 1940. *House and Fulani Proverbs.* Lagos: Nigerian Government.
Wiggins, William H. 1971. "Jack Johnson as Bad Nigger." *The Black Scholar* 2, no. 5, 35-46.
Wildavsky, Aaron. 1984a. "From Political Economy to Political Culture or Rational People Defend Their Way of Life." Paper delivered at annual meeting of the American Political Science Association, Washington, D.C.
——. 1984b. *The Nursing Father: Moses as a Political Leader.* University, Alabama: University of Alabama Press.
Wilkins, Roger. 1984. "Demos Shouldn't Go Cold-hearted." *The Oakland Tribune,* 22 November.
Willhelm, Sidney M. 1979. "Martin Luther King, Jr. and the Black Experience in America." *Journal of Black Studies* 10, no. 1 (September), 3-19.
Williams, Chancellor. 1976. *The Destruction of Black Civilization.* Chicago: Third World Press.
Williams, John A. 1970. *The King God Didn't Save: Reflections on the Life & Death of Martin Luther King.* New York: Coward, McCann and Geoghegan.
William, Linda Faye. 1977. "Race, Class and Politics: The Impact of American Political Economy on Black Detroit." Unpublished Ph.D. diss., University of Chicago.
Williams, Margaret. 1982. "National Baptist Leader Unseated." *The Call and Post,* Columbus, Ohio, 25 September.
Williams, Melvin D. 1974. *Community in a Black Pentecostal Church.* Pittsburgh: University of Pittsburgh Press.
Willingham, Alex. 1975. "Ideology and Politics: Their Status in Afro-American Social Theory." *ENDARCH* 1, no. 2 (Spring).
——. 1981. "The Place of the New Black Conservatives in Black Social Thought." Paper presented at annual meeting of the Association for the Study of Afro-American Life and History, Philadelphia, October.
Willner, Ann Ruth. 1984. *The Spellbinders.* New Haven: Yale University Press.
Wills, Gary. 1979. *Confessions of a Conservative.* New York: Doubleday.
Wilmore, Gayraud S. 1973. *Black Religion and Black Radicalism.* Garden City, New York: Anchor.
——, and James H. Cone, eds. 1979. *Black Theology.* Maryknoll, New York: Orbis.
Wilson, James Q. 1960. *Negro Politics.* Glencoe: The Free Press.
——. 1973. *Political Organizations.* New York: Basic Books.
Wilson, John F. 1979. *Public Religion in American Culture.* Philadelphia: Temple University Press.
Wilson, Ortiz. 1972. *Music: Black, White, & Blue.* New York: Morrow.

Wilson, William Julius. 1978. *The Declining Significance of Race.* Chicago: University of Chicago Press.

—. 1979. "The Declining Significance of Race: Myth or Reality." Denison University lecture, 25 April.

Winston, Henry. 1973. *Strategy for a Black Agenda.* New York: International.

Wolin, Sheldon S. 1960. *Politics and Vision.* Boston: Little, Brown.

—. 1982. "America's Civil Religion." *Democracy* 2, no. 2 (April).

Wolters, Raymond. 1970. *Negroes and the Great Depression.* Westport, Connecticut: Greenwood.

Woodson, Carter G., ed. 1942. *The Works of Francis J. Grimke.* Washington: Associated Publishers.

Wright, Nathan, Jr. 1968. *Let's Work Together.* New York: Hawthorn.

—. 1972. *What Black Politicians Are Saying.* New York: Hawthorn.

Zinn, Howard. 1964. *SNCC: The New Abolitionists.* Boston: Beacon.

Zolberg, Aristide, and Vera Zolberg. 1967. "The Americanization of Frantz Fanon." *The Public Interest* 9 (Fall).

Index

Affirmative action: black neoconservatives, 101

Africa: nonliteracy and political organization, 8; folk culture and black traditionalism, 14–19; origins of blues, 30–31; independence and religion, 74–75; Marxism and colonial theory, 103–105

Afro-American culture: oral tradition and black ideology, 7–8; post–Civil War, 19–22; origins of blues, 30; colonial theory, 105–109

Aggression: black and white cultural styles, 44–45

American Creed: black and white perceptions, 2; definition, 111n

Art and artists: value conflicts and cultural dominance, 10–11; creative freedom, 29–30; blues as, 30–33; vision and revolution, 38–39

Bad men: Afro-American folk tales, 48–51; Afro-American style and lower-class behavior, 58–59; tradition and rejection of authority, 93–94

Bandit: white and black bad man, 51

Baptist Church: black sermons, 83

Bebop: political change and the blues, 26

Bible: slave revolts, 45; black preachers and current events, 65; traditional Afro-American sermon, 85

Black power: redemptive suffering, 69–73; King and nonviolence, 73–74; European ideologies, 104

Black studies: academic field and literature, 3; neoconservative opposition, 96–97

Blues: black ideology and language, 8; class and social deviance, 13; post–Civil War culture, 21–22; culture and ideology, 22–23; sexual themes and black culture, 23–24; decline in sixties, 24; as protest, 25–30; as art, 30–33; revolutionary character, 57–58; individuality, 113n

Bradley, Tom: leadership style, 43, 44; white support, 89

Charisma: black leadership, 85–88

Church, black: functions, 63; black tradition and civil rights movement, 75; Jackson, 88, 89

Civic religion: Puritanism, 61; Garvey and language, 63–64; Garvey and King, 70;

black church tradition, 75; traditional white denominations, 91; black challenge to status quo, 91–92; Jackson campaign and black version, 92

Civil rights movement: political systems and organizations, 43; King on Garvey, 69–70

Civil War: Afro-American culture, 19

Class: language and political thought, 9–10; culture and social deviance, 12–14; religious affiliation and style of musical performance, 21; lyrics of blues songs, 27; decline in popularity of blues, 33; black culture and music, 35–36; black leadership and militancy, 41; lower-class behavior and black politics, 54; neoconservatives and black progress, 101, 102

Colonialism: community and culture, 102–103; Marxism and Africa, 103–105; Afro-American perspective, 105–109

Communication: racial groups, 1; symbols and black political thought, 4

Community: individual and cultural fragmentation, 95–96; blacks and corporations, 98; colonialism and culture, 102–103; black politics and colonial theory, 106

Cone, James: violence and theology, 70–72; nationalism and theology, 115n

Conservatism: black traditionalism, 14–15; moral hegemony and values, 101

Cool jazz: political change and the blues, 26

Corporations: black Reaganites, 97–98

Crime: as political protest, 48; violence and black folklore, 52

Crummell, Alexander: Garvey and black religious tradition, 64, 65

Culture: language development and black political thought, 9; upper-class deviant, 12–13; class and social pathology, 13–14; post–Civil War, 19–22; blues, 22–25; rap music, 33–35; lower-class black Americans, 35–36; vision of America as entity, 95–96; community and colonialism, 102–103; colonial theory, 104

Dance: origins of blues, 31; black prejudice against secular, 113n

Dawson, William: leadership style, 41, 43

Debate: black and white cultural norms, 44

Decentralization: black politics and community control, 106